BSTYLED for life

LIVING WITH SASS AND STYLE OVER 50

MOANA ROBINSON

First published by Ultimate World Publishing 2019
Copyright © 2019 Moana Robinson

ISBN

Paperback - 978-1-925884-71-5
eBook - 978-1-925884-72-2

Moana Robinson has asserted her right under the Copyright, Designs and Patents Act 1988 to be identified as the author of this work. The information in this book is based on the author's experiences and opinions. The publisher specifically disclaims responsibility for any adverse consequences, which may result from use of the information contained herein. Permission to use information has been sought by the author. Any breaches will be rectified in further editions of the book.

All rights reserved. No part of this publication may be reproduced, stored in or introduced into a retrieval system, or transmitted in any form, or by any means (electronic, mechanical, photocopying, recording or otherwise) without the prior written permission of the author. Any person who does any unauthorised act in relation to this publication may be liable to criminal prosecution and civil claims for damages. Enquiries should be made through the publisher.

Cover design: Ultimate World Publishing
Photography: Sumico Photography
Icon design from Iconfinder.com
Illustrations: Jen and Jennifer
Layout and typesetting: Ultimate World Publishing
Editor: Felicity Frankish

Ultimate World Publishing
Diamond Creek,
Victoria Australia 3089
www.writeabook.com.au

TESTIMONIALS

I've personally known Moana Robinson for nine years now and she is one of those women who is a rare find. She's true to her word, loyal, tenacious, hard-working and a giver. Her passion for helping her clients shines through with everything she does. Having many successful businesses, a big family, travelling and all the ups and downs of life, I have no doubt this book will help so many women face anything in life, as Moana has personally and professionally been through so much. She has always amazed me at how she just picks herself up and keeps going. I'm sure a huge part of this is her drive to serve others. She's a stunning woman on the outside, but it's what she's done to develop herself on the inside over the years that has made her the incredible woman she is today that I'm honoured to call my friend.

**Shar Moore, CEO/Founder Y Mag® Magazine,
Australia's Leading Magazine for the Thinking Woman**

Moana is hot! When you look at this beautiful, mature, sexy woman you can be tricked into thinking she's a woman who has it all: blessed, lucky and fortunate. Moana is a bright, intelligent and intuitive woman, who combines her knowledge of style and beauty care with mental care, to craft a whole healthy woman. She is soft, gentle and wise. She smiles with her eyes and looks deep into your soul to bring out the best in every woman, so they can shine from inside out. She makes every woman feel beautiful and you'll get caught up in her magnificent glow.

**Barbara Clifford,
Time Management Strategist, The Time Tamer**

If you are over 50 and have a personality that your body and wardrobe don't match – talk to Moana. She's so helpful, knowledgeable and approachable, and very genuinely wants you to shine! Moana's knowledge of colour and fabrics, her eye for spectacular outfits that suit YOU and her wonderfully warm humanity hug you while she helps you to understand what looks good on you and what doesn't. When you're feeling good on the inside, it shows, so let Moana help your personality shine!

Valerie O'Neill, Owner at Ask Valerie

Beauty is more than our external appearance. Beauty is our confidence and self-worth. These are seen and felt by all. To find someone who understands and fosters this with those around her, and who has written a book that reinforces this message, is brilliant. Moana has created something well worth reading.

Tracie Eaton, Professional Artist @ Tracie Eaton

It's wonderful that Moana has created a book to help women who have reached an age where sometimes they may be starting on a new journey of self-discovery. With her styling and coaching knowledge and experience, she is able to share information in a concise and easy-to-follow guide, which also draws on challenges that I personally know she has had and overcome. She provided style to some clients who needed professional advice on what to wear at my 50 over 50 project – portraits of 50 women over the age of 50. It helped them to feel good and confident on their choice of outfits for their photo session. She always provides great advice with a positive manner. She helps women feel and look great.

**Sumiko Eyears,
Sumico Photography, Creator of 50 over 50 Project**

DEDICATION

For my sister Ruth

For my mum Pamela

For my daughters Dayna and Molly

*For
all women
looking
outside
for something that is right there
inside,
this body of possibility we call "self"*

*For all men
who are aware
of the possibilities
within the women they know and love*

*For
the heart and soul
of sass and style,
right here
right now,
which is
YOU*

FOREWORD

As a man approaching 50, I was curious and honoured when Moana (I call her Mo) asked me to pen a foreword for her first book.

In my passion and purpose coaching practice, I've worked with hundreds of women from 16 to 65 discover what kindles their spark for life, and what reignites passions within them, which might have been dimmed over the course of time, trials and tribulations.

To understand that whatever their journeys have been…new paths and detours can be forked, nurtured and styled to live the best life that they want – a full and rich life.

I recall my early days of training to be a coach.

One early morning in sunny Brisbane, I walked into a room filled with aspiring coaches for the first day of hypnotherapy training.

Unsure of what the day might bring, I scanned the room for my first connection, searching for the first willing and friendly face.

What caught my eye was a magnetically beautiful woman.

Aesthetically stylish, for sure, but most definitely, a beautiful woman!

But wait…

Also energetically peaceful with kind eyes.

When I subsequently worked with this lady, Mo, in our coaching drills, my suspicions were confirmed.

A beautiful, peaceful *and* kind woman. Despite what seemed like a discomfort in her back when she adjusted her frame intermittently during our coaching sessions, she was resolute in her determination to complete our coaching drills.

Beautiful, peaceful, kind *and* determined!

We've grown to be friends and colleagues ever since.

It wasn't until much later that I found out Mo had cysts in the nerves of her spine and sacral area, and that she'd been plagued by chronic pain and had been on extremely strong painkillers the entire time.

Beautiful, peaceful, kind, determined *and* empowered!

Over the years, Mo has both professionally and personally, looked into the eyes of her strongest fears, trials and tribulations with love, compassion and a mindset of learning, growing and evolving.

"If we feel good, we look good. If we look good, we feel good."

With Mo, I would add… "If we feel and look good, we do good".

I've seen Mo grow her personal stylist and life coaching business from strength to strength, working with both men and women alike.

I've been excited to be part of her *Take A MOment* live videos encouraging everyone to take a moment to reflect, re-focus and re-energise.

Foreword

Her most recent gift to her local community is the *Tuesdays on Tedder group* on the Gold Coast, designed to inspire, support and empower aspiring local entrepreneurs.

In Mo's book, you will find the loving ingredients to a recipe for appreciating and empowering yourself to beauty – a pathway to discover, create and fashion your unique style from the inside out.

We've all heard it.

As I write this foreword, I'm inspired!

Mo, in her own special unique style, makes me feel connected to her stories. Her narratives touch the heart, mind and soul.

I'm excited to read the finished product!

Andrew Low

Andrew Low
The Passion and Purpose Coach
Andrew Low Coaching and Training

CONTENTS

Testimonials	iii
Dedication	vii
Foreword	ix
Introduction	xv

PART 1 – THE INSIDE

Chapter 1. Best Time Of Your Life	3
Chapter 2. Birds And The Bees	17
Chapter 3. Becoming	27
Chapter 4. Believing	39
Chapter 5. Balancing Your Life	49

PART 2 – THE OUTSIDE

Chapter 6. Booties, Boobies And Other Bits	63
Chapter 7. Being You	79
Chapter 8. Bold And Beautiful	93
Chapter 9. Black Is Not A Colour	105
Chapter 10. Benefits Of Choice	117
Chapter 11. Be A Smart And Sassy Shopper	129
Chapter 12. Brilliant Life And Style Tips	135

About The Author	139
Acknowledgements	141
Testimonials (Contd)	143
Free Style Guide	147
Special Consultation	149
Speaking Engagements	151

INTRODUCTION

When you look at me who do you see?
Who are you to label me?
Am I defined by the child I birth,
or does my career define my worth?
The curves on my body, the marks on my skin
the scratch on the surface of this vessel I'm in.
Am I defined by the food I eat?
The tiny wins or the crushing defeats?
Do you see my tolerance wearing thin,
or the shame and the pain buried deep within?
When you look at me who do you see?
Me or who you think I should be?
The length of my hair, the breadth of my thighs,
the laughter or the tears in my eyes?
Do the scales represent my strength or resolve?
Do my scars mean I'm broken or whole?
Do my beliefs define my mind,
or who I was in one moment in time.
Do you see my chains or my beautiful wings,
because I am all and none of these things.
When you look at me who do you see?
You see more of you than you do of me.

- **Untamed Poetess**

Why have I written this book? The simple answer – because I wanted to. This is a project I really wanted to start and finish. There is a huge amount of satisfaction in starting and finishing something. Throughout my life there have been projects, which I started and then put off finishing because 'life' gets in the way. It's important to me that I package up some of the information and discoveries I have made to date.

Some of us take a longer time to get to do what we want to do. I've raised a family and helped start a successful family business. I've worked full-time and part time, studied and created my own business, and I'm continually learning. At this age, I have a burning desire to carry through with something I thought about as a child. Life is a journey full of discoveries. We discover so much about ourselves as we get older. This stage of life suits the description the 'Wisdom Years'. I'm well into and almost through my 50s at the time of writing this book and feel so much passion about it. I'm excited I finally get to do what I thought about all those years ago.

Stages Of Life

I remember my aunt, who was very special to me, saying she felt like she'd lived three lifetimes in one. As I get older I understand what she meant. Life is made up of several stages. We get the chance to refresh and renew at the beginning of each stage.

As a 10 year old, I was walking home from school thinking I'd like to write a book one day. Isn't it amazing that we can remember some thoughts we had at 10 years old and then as we get older, we can't remember what we had for lunch yesterday!

I hope this book will help people refresh and renew themselves. I've been inspired by others and would like, in turn, to inspire other people. To be inspiring, we first need to be inspired ourselves.

Introduction

If We Feel Good, We Look Good

I've always had an interest in helping others and have always loved fashion – beautiful clothes, art and connecting with people. Incorporating these interests into the business side came about after the age of 50. Personal styling is something I'd always thought about getting into, and as a personal stylist, I found myself telling people, "I'm not interested in just the outside image. I want to help people feel good on the inside as well". The poem at the start of this book describes perfectly what perception is all about. We can't see something in others unless we recognise it and it's somewhere in us as well. Style is about who we are, not who others think we should be.

Both aspects of 'B Styled for Life' were born out of a desire to help people feel good about themselves, as well as look good.

"If we feel good we look good, and if we look good we feel good."

It's like a circle. It all has a flow-on effect. If we endeavour to be the best we can be, it has a ripple effect on those around us.

This book is written for women looking for that different outlook on life. There will always be someone who is worse off than ourselves. There will always be someone who is better off health-wise, financially and every which way. Who is the judge of being 'better off' though? The important point to remember is that we constantly strive to be the best person for ourselves and those we care about.

I've made some extremely tough personal choices in life, which have turned out to be good choices. There are so many aspects of life to write about. This book will be the catalyst for me to write more. 'B Styled for Life – Living with Sass and Style Over 50' is a collection of my learnings over the past few years. I am appreciative of the support of the Academy of Professional Image, who I have been able to contact from time to time. The Life Coaching College has also provided a wonderful platform with excellent trainers to support and springboard coaching professionals. I wondered how to incorporate the coaching and styling into my business and find that both skills work in conjunction with each other. This gives me plenty of variety and a lot of understanding about human nature and personalities. My business is evolving into something very unique. This book provides a base from which I can expand my services to further support my clients and a wider audience.

Two Parts

The first part of this book is devoted to the 'inside' and the second part to the practical aspects of styling/image, or the 'outside' of women at this very special next stage of life.

The title 'Sass and Style' came about, because by the time a woman has reached her 50s, she has developed a certain amount of sass. To reach these years there has to be a certain amount of self-awareness and self-sufficiency. My goal is to give you some simple tools for style, confidence and other aspects of life.

In earlier years, we are still discovering ourselves and learning about the world around us. Life is often a lot simpler then, and yet also quite complex, because many experiences are first times. The 'Wisdom Years' stage provides women over 50 with experience and a kind of 'knowing' that it can all be ok, because so far we have made it through. It takes guts and courage to do some things when we are younger, such as skydive, take up a sporting challenge, start a business, get married, take out a mortgage, buy a property and raise a family. It also takes guts and courage later in life to reinvent yourself. To become a woman who is prepared to fight for the life she wants and is prepared to stand tall and be the person she wants to be. As a woman over 50, you deserve to be the you that you want to be. This is the case at any age, and I hope that women over 50 reading this book will also pass it on to younger women.

Introduction

Truth And Honesty

Being true to yourself is one of the most important things you can do in life. If you aren't true to yourself, how can you be true and honest with other people? There's no race and it doesn't matter what you're doing in life. It does matter who you are being. The most important person you can be is you. Take stock of your age and start, right now, being and doing what is right for you.

So many of my friends have discovered their passion later in life. They have done the 'first stage' and maybe the 'second stage' and now it is time for 'act 3' of the life story. One of my dear friends Sumiko (Sumi), who took the photograph for the cover of this book, used to say at our business mastermind meetings that she had been practising photography and really loved it. She said that one day she would like to do more photography, but her website and graphic art business paid the bills and she needed to focus on that. Two years down the track she is now a multi award-winning photographer who is about to hold her exhibition of 50 Women Over the age of 50 titled '50 Over 50'. I'm so proud of her and her achievements. She helped me create my first website years ago for personal styling and took some glamour photographs of me at a very pivotal time in my life.

One Of The Toughest And Best Choices – The Start of A Journey

In November 2015, I had a session booked with Sumi to get some photographs taken for my styling business. The day before, I had received the news that I had Tarlov Cysts in the nerves of my spine and sacral area, which were too risky to operate on. The pain had been chronic and the issue had been masked by a synovial cyst, which had been operated on the previous year. I went along to the photoshoot with tears in my eyes. I felt alone and scared. There seemed to be no neurosurgeon in Australia who was willing to help. If left, the condition had the chance of eroding the sacral bones and I would have to be on extremely strong painkillers for the rest of my life. Thanks to the photoshoot that morning, Sumi was the first one of my friends to know about this from the beginning. I look at those photographs, knowing that choosing to have surgery with a Dallas neurosurgeon in Cyprus turned out to be one of those 'good' choices. I'm grateful Sumi took those photographs for me. As a woman over 50 herself, she has been able to inspire other women by photographing them in a way that is unique and beautiful. Sumi said she gains just as much inspiration from her clients as they do from being photographed in such a special way. Now the photography keeps her extremely busy and she is on her second round of applications for 50 women over the age of 50 to photograph. How wonderful that someone can turn her love of photography into the ability to make women feel so good about themselves. These women always say it's more than a glamour photo session, they actually "discover more about themselves".

By A Woman For Women

Many of my friends are fulfilling their goals and dreams. The way women support each other is so powerful. I'm not excluding men here, as many men, including my wonderful, generous and caring husband, are also so inspirational. This book is written for women, because as a woman, I have been through the ups and downs, the feelings of "not good enough", or even "not enough" and "not doing enough". As a mum and now grandmother, I realise this is achieved by just being me and doing the best I can. Lessons have been learnt along the way and I'm now grateful for them.

Your Goals And Dreams

Two of my favourite things to do are connecting and sharing. I'm connecting all the dots of everything I have learnt and putting it in this book. I'm sharing it with you, because every woman should have the opportunity to live their life fulfilling their goals and dreams.

Introduction

You Can Start Right Now

This book is not only for women over 50 – it is for all women (and men too) to realise that as you go through different stages and ages, you can start right here, right now, to be the best person you can be. It is the unique you who has sass and style, and no-one can take that away. With self-awareness and self-sufficiency (knowing you can do what you want to do and that you can ask for help) the next day, week, month and years can be the best time of your life.

Oceans Of Possibilities

I hope it helps you and yours. I hope women who read this book realise there are oceans of possibilities for you. I hope it gives you the knowledge and inspiration to be the best person that you can possibly be – a woman with your own unique version of sass and style!

Part 1
THE INSIDE

1.
Best Time of Your Life

"You are never too old to set another goal or to dream a new dream."

- C.S. Lewis

Years ago, being over 50 was classed as middle-aged. It's probably more true these days than it ever was, because we are living longer. Times are different now and we don't really talk about age the same way. What really is middle aged? We don't know how long we're going to live. We could live until next week, next month, next year, or the next 10 years, 20 years, 30 years. It's an unknown. All we have is today, right now, and my motto has always been, "Today is the first day of the rest of your life, make it the best of your life".

Inspiration

We all know someone who is an inspiration to us. Someone who even in their older years has been willing to learn something new, has a zest for life and a great sense of humour. I have quite a few examples, some being my clients. I respect and admire them for taking an interest in how they look on the outside, and for the interest they take on their personal development even after the age of 50.

People I see in news articles inspire me. A couple of days ago, I read about Lorna Prendergast who was 90 years old, graduating from the University of Melbourne. Lorna comes from a town about 300 kilometres east of Melbourne. She hopes that by speaking about her experience of returning to study, others will realise you're never too old to learn. I believe that by learning, we take the focus off ourselves, even with some of the health ailments we may have, and turn our focus onto the outside world. This broadens our outlook on life.

Good, Better, Best

It's definitely possible to feel the best you've ever felt, and to look absolutely fantastic after the age of 50. I feel better now in my 50s than I ever felt in my 30s or 40s.

> *"Good, better, best, never let it rest, till your good is better, and your better is best."*
>
> **– St Jerome**

Why can't these years be some of the best years of your life? The combination of all the struggles you have had – the highs, the lows, the in-betweens – contribute to you being wiser, more confident and feeling better in yourself than you've ever felt before.

There is nothing to stop you from going for what you want. Age is just a number. Some people have a better attitude at 50 than others do at 30 or 20. It almost feels that after you turn 50, you finally grow up. You've grown into yourself and have evolved personally. You understand more about yourself and, in turn, you understand more about other people. With this understanding and knowledge, relationships are improved. You develop a kind of quiet confidence knowing you are doing the best you possibly can in each circumstance.

The Occasional Cha Cha

Sure, life can throw you some curve balls, and you can be challenged daily. The exciting part is that as a more mature woman, you can handle those challenges, because you have before. I realise now that mindset is so important. If you have a positive mindset, and look at the positive side of things, it makes such a huge difference. Even if you do the 'cha cha' occasionally and take two steps back before you take one step forward – if you remind yourself that it is all to do with mindset – you will get through whatever challenges come.

Some of the key benefits that I see from growing older:

Confidence And Knowledge
Being a mature-aged woman, you have more confidence. Confidence comes from experience. It comes from positive thinking and putting that positive thinking into practice. It comes from knowledge. It comes from connection. It comes from talking to other people and discovering that they sometimes feel the same way you do. Time is good to us and has given us a sense of knowing through discovery and just living life.

Confidence comes from feelings of wellbeing, acceptance of your body and your mind, your self-esteem, and belief in your own ability, skills and experience. You know you have been through some tough times, and you're still here. You've come out the other side wiser and more confident.

> *"Waiting for circumstances to change so you can feel good is like looking in a mirror waiting for your reflection to smile first."*
> **– Bashar**

Plenty To Love

We can't love other people if we don't love ourselves first. The capacity to love is within us all. The most important person to love is yourself. We can always love others as well. The benefit of loving at this age is that most of us have loved more people by now and have more people to love. We know that feeling of being in love and that feeling of loving. After so many years, we have also learnt about discernment and who is worthy of our time, care and attention. This is one of the biggest lessons I've learnt being in my 50s. Now, I'm very discerning about who I spend my time with. I'm discerning about who I trust, I'm also very conscious about how important it is to look after the people you love and to appreciate the good people in life. There's plenty to love about life and the opportunities you've had and still have.

Understanding And Awareness

Understanding yourself comes with age, as does understanding your feelings, your emotions and accepting that these are all part of life.

By now we are more understanding with other people and realise that everyone is fighting some kind of battle. We are also self-aware. Being aware of your own characteristics and personality is empowering. This helps you become aware of other people and what is going on around you.

I no longer think of being in your 50s as old. I no longer think of 60s, 70s, or 80s as old. It is just an age. In some ways, being older frees you up, as you are more self-aware. You're more conscious about why you think a certain way and why you take certain actions. When you are younger, you don't even think about it. You just take the actions and your life carries on.

Chapter 1 - Best Time Of Your Life

"Once you know who you really are, being is enough. You feel neither superior to anyone nor inferior to anyone and you have no need for approval because you've awakened to your own infinite worth."

- Deepak Chopra

Road To Wisdom

All aspects of your life lead to the top of this road, which is classed as wisdom. Sometimes it takes us this long to evolve. We learn to take notice of our intuition. We learn not to be so concerned about what other people think. We learn to take action. If we don't take action, we often experience severe regret. We learn to manage our state. If we don't manage our state or our emotions, we introduce or encourage drama into our life. We learn about decision-making and problem-solving through events in our lives. We understand the habits we've developed over the years, and we learn that we can actually break those habits and overcome compulsions we may have.

Your Most Valuable Asset

Health is your number one priority – your greatest asset. Self-care is very important. We've all heard the analogy about the oxygen mask and the airplane. If you don't put that oxygen mask on yourself, how can you ever help other people? I'm still learning that I'm not a machine, and I still have very high expectations of myself. At the same time, I am enjoying life now more than I ever have before. A lot of this is because of my age and a sense of appreciation for health, people and opportunities.

Sense Of Humour

I know the value of having fun in your life. How good does it feel to have friends you can laugh and share a joke with? The eternal truth is that "laughter is one of the best medicines". It's when we take life, and ourselves, too seriously that we seem to get 'older' or dragged down. One of the greatest attributes my mum has is her great sense of humour. She laughs at herself and we have great conversations, which are enjoyable and fun.

Pride And Experience

Speaking of Mum, I'm extremely proud of her. She's in her 90s and using the internet, learning French and has overcome many challenges. Mum kept her memoirs for 40 or so years and belonged to a writing group. Talking about this with me is something which contributed to my thoughts on writing a book. She learned how to paint in later years, too. I have some of her paintings, which are beautiful, floral watercolours.

I'm proud of who I am and I want you to be proud of yourself, too. If you're younger than 50, I want you to know there is a time to look forward to when you can put all the experiences of your life together. You can look back and realise how much those experiences have taught you.

I'd like my daughters to be proud of me, not for what I've achieved, but for the person that I am. I'd like to inspire them to do what they want to do and to follow their heart. Have you ever thought about wanting to do something, and thinking, "I'm too old to start this"? We all know the global fast-food chain KFC. Colonel Sanders didn't start until he was 65 years old. All you need is confidence, self-belief, and some support from your family and friends. Even if you don't get support, take negative comments as fuel to carry and live the life you want to live. We come into this world alone, and we die alone, so our life is ours to live.

Look for the lesson in each experience, even ones that brought you to your knees and cut into your heart so deeply that you thought you could never recover. I want you to remember that each and every person has had these types of experiences. They might not talk about it, but no human can go through life and smooth sail the whole way along. It's as though when you turn 50, everything finally comes into alignment if you allow it. Step back and take notice of what has happened in your life. Take notice of how you feel each day and just become curious. Treat yourself like a project. This is one of the most exciting times of your life.

Whatever it is that you want to do, don't do it to prove something to anyone else: do it for yourself. Think about what you've always had a passion for and just do it. That's why I love the Nike slogan, 'Just Do It'. It's very powerful, it's very simple, and it says it as it is.

Connection

Connection is another way we can keep feeling good, active and wanting to learn more. Through exposure to other people, we learn more, and as we share and collaborate, other people can learn from us, too.

As a society, we need to be connected with other people. It's great to have time by yourself, but also able to just pick up the phone and connect with people when you need to.

New Start

Every day is a chance to make a new start. An opportunity to change something you don't like into something you do like. Take baby steps, just one at a time, towards what it is you want to achieve.

New Opportunities

No matter what age you are, it's important that you're your own best friend, best coach, and best cheer squad. There's nothing wrong with asking for help or support from family and friends. You can also seek advice from professional coaches and mentors. Ultimately though, it's up to you. You might be heading towards retirement, or retired now, but we still need to work on ourselves all the time. We still need to look at how our days are going, and we can still give back to society in some way.

I'm amazed at the number of young people in their 20s or 30s, who are wondering if it's too late to start doing something, like learn a musical instrument or take up a new sport. It's never too late. If you really want to do something, do it. If your physical abilities limit you, then do something else. If we could easily have everything and easily do everything that we wanted, life would be boring. It wouldn't give us any challenges. If there's something you really want to do, try it and see if it works. If you can't do it because of your physical restrictions, just face up to it and be happy. Try something else.

I'd wanted to take up running before I had my two back surgeries. I was advised not to go running, and I've faced up to that. I go to Pilates instead and love it. I really want you to look at the positives of getting older. As we get older, we have more patterns in place which create consistency for ourselves. We have experiences to draw on. We have more wisdom.

The Attitude Of A Learner

What I have focused on is becoming open to learning. There are some things I don't want to take into my world, and other things that I look at and have a sense of curiosity to learn more about. I've noticed when going to networking events, a lot of older women are starting to attend, which is fantastic. A great learner is someone who's independent and doesn't expect someone else to give it to them on a plate. They enjoy learning. They are enthusiastic, confident and determined to get there. A great learner isn't someone who is comparing themselves to other people. They see other people who know more and strive to learn more. They have a sense of curiosity.

Many Benefits

I spoke to a woman recently who is around 80 years old. She told me she can't run up the stairs anymore, she forgets her passwords, and she has trouble reaching her toes to cut her toenails. But she said the last 20 or 30 years have been the best part of her life. She has memories and imagination. She's learned to be more patient and to enjoy quietness and space. She has shared love and closeness with her family, and all the young people around her, so she believes being older is pretty good.

Three Intricate Stages

Yes, we have different stages of our lives. We start out when we're born, being an empty slate, and develop as we go along. It's what we do with our life that creates the world that we have now. By the time you get to this stage of your life, you may feel like you've lived three lifetimes in one, especially if you've moved countries like I have, if you've raised a family, if you've been through a lot of life challenges. Whatever your first stage looked like: it could be that you've had different relationships, career changes and moves. Lots of different things contribute to this feeling of living a few different lifetimes. All these experiences make life more interesting. I think of it like a tapestry, or an intricate design on a piece of material. It all contributes to the strength of that piece of material, the interest in it, and the attractiveness to look at.

When my daughters were young, I used to say to my mother-in-law each year, "I think this is the best age right now". Now that I'm in my 50s about to turn 60, I feel that from now on each year is the very best year of my life, and I will keep on having that attitude. There's a huge difference between living and merely existing. The main point is it's your life to live. As long as you are happy and healthy, and living a life that's honest with yourself, and honest with others, I believe you are living your best life right now.

Beauty Is Ageless

You are beautiful. Who says that beauty needs to be youthful? Beauty is in the eye of the beholder and is how you feel. Is there a rule that says, "I am 50 now. I need to dress like an older woman, I need to downplay my appearance, I need to dull myself down, I need to not shine, I need to disappear and become invisible"? If you are using these words on yourself, listen to your self-talk and distinguish whose voice you are hearing. It may not even be your voice! It could be society and what you have read somewhere, or heard, or been told when you were a child. You could be following the example of someone else who turned 50 and kept saying they were no longer beautiful because they were old. Change your language and realise your own beauty. Talk to yourself as you would talk to your own loved child or best friend. Look in the mirror every morning and see your own beauty. Words are powerful. I challenge you to look in the mirror every day and say, "You are beautiful". You have the benefit of knowing all these things at this age. Use healthy, positive language about yourself and remind yourself there is no age limit to beauty.

> *"You have been criticising yourself for years and it hasn't worked. Try approving of yourself and see what happens."*
> - **Louise Hay**

As Time Flies By

Each year, Christmas seems to come around faster and faster. It seems that we blink and the year has gone by.

Chapter 1 - Best Time Of Your Life

As we get older, sometimes we complain about how fast time goes. You know that the time only drags if you're not having fun. Change that to a positive – time is going fast, because we're having fun, we're living a full life and we are appreciating every single day.

No Regrets

Have no regrets. If you feel time has been wasted, there's no such thing. If you've been resting, you needed that rest. If you've been working hard, you've reaped the rewards for it. If you've made mistakes, you've learned from those mistakes. One of the benefits of this time of your life is living more in the present, being grateful for what you have, and being appreciative for the lessons you've learned.

Action Steps

1. Take a look at a photograph of yourself from 20 years ago. Be objective. Look at that photograph without being critical and without paying attention to the hair style or the clothing. Think of yourself as the person you were at that age. Then take a look at yourself in the mirror and say you feel proud of you. Feel proud of how far you've come, where you've come from and what you've done during those years. I want you to appreciate who you are and talk to yourself as though you are your own best friend, or your own daughter.

2. Write in a journal. Write about yourself in a loving, appreciative, grateful way for how you've come to where you are now. Have some quiet time to yourself. I've only just discovered writing in a journal in the last two years. It really is so cathartic. It releases your emotions and frees you up to think of new ideas.

3. Make a list of all the benefits you can think of that come with being the age you are right now. For example: can spoil my grandchildren, no more periods, lower or no mortgage, pensioner discounts, etc…

Chapter 1 - Best Time Of Your Life

Resources

Great link for an online journal to make notes as mentioned in point number two, if you prefer to keep a secret stash of love notes to yourself! https://www.penzu.com

2. Birds and the Bees

Your Nest

You've possibly raised your family, they've grown up, left home and you may be suffering from what's called the "Empty Nest Syndrome". It's a new stage of your life. You have the house to yourself, you can start new interests. Your relationship with your partner could be significantly changing. This is the time to adjust or adapt to the changes, while also concentrating on your relationship with yourself.

Regardless of your family situation, this stage also brings about friendship changes as people move away or retire, or you change where you live and what you do on a day-to-day basis. The whole dynamic of life is always changing and it's a matter of adapting to those changes.

Your Most Important Relationship

In our 20s, 30s and even 40s, we were only just discovering all about our relationships with other people. Now is the time for you to focus more on yourself. The relationship with yourself is the most important one you can ever have.

You also know by now what is acceptable and unacceptable in a relationship. You know what works and what doesn't work. The most important part of any relationship is communication. The title of this chapter is 'The Birds and the Bees'. According to Wikipedia, the 'birds and the bees' is an English-language idiomatic expression and euphemism that refers to courtship and sexual intercourse. The 'birds and the bees talk', as it used to be known, is the event in most children's lives when their parents explain what sexual relationships are.

By the time you reach this age, whether you are in a relationship or not, personal development and relationship development talks are something every person, and every couple, needs to have. As much as young children need to know about the birds and the bees, we all need to learn about personal and relationship development throughout various stages of life.

Personal Development And Relationship Development

Apply the following ideas for close social relationships, as well as intimate relationships – the basics are similar.

Being in a good personal relationship helps you feel you have a stable home environment, with support and connection. Being in a good relationship helps you become the person you want to be. It's great to have someone with you who cares for you and other people. You need to be able to have fun with your significant other. You need fulfillment in a relationship. The same is true of your relationship with yourself – you need to feel fulfilled in life. It's important to have shared experiences and also independent experiences. It's important to have a sense of belonging and a sense of community, as well as a sense of being part of something bigger than yourself. A fantastic, intimate relationship and social relationships help relieve stress, as you are provided with support and made to feel good.

Chapter 2 - Birds And The Bees

Stress Sucks

Stress is something I feel very strongly about. It can be insidious. There is normal positive stress that is part of day-to-day life. However, negative stress that is unrelenting and chronic is damaging and can lead to adrenal fatigue, severe depression and anxiety. Stress can suck the life out of a relationship. It can do so much damage to physical, emotional and mental health. Whatever you can do to reduce stress, especially at this time of life, you need to do it. Make sure your relationships and your connections are positive ones and have people in your world who you want in your world.

A lot of business people suffer a tremendous amount of stress. It's important to remind yourself and other people how much you appreciate them. Connection, communication and appreciation are important in any relationship, along with honesty and openness. Management of stress is something not to be taken lightly and there's a lot of wonderful help now to assist with techniques to reduce stress.

Good Habits

It's important there is give and take in a relationship. This goes for your significant other and also your social relationships. Sharing a desire to be healthy with your partner will lead to a healthy diet and exercise, which promotes a fulfilling and healthy life. Develop some daily habits that you can do together. It could be going for walks, catching up for a meal or sharing an interest. Something my husband and I have always done to start the day off right is to make the bed together. He does complain about the number of pillows and cushions on our bed, and I've heard this is a standing joke with other couples as well!

Social Connection

People who have strong social connections, as well as people to care for and who care for them, are more likely to live longer than those who are more isolated. Even if you do live by yourself, make the effort to get out, get connected and have an active social life.

Social contact is important for everyone. A study conducted and published in PLOS Medicine reported that social contact could also play an important role in staving off dementia. This is a strong reason to promote connected communities and find ways to reduce isolation and loneliness.

Ebbs And Flows

Life, just like relationships, has the ebbs and flows. Life would be boring if we didn't have challenges. It's how we handle the challenges that makes the difference. In any relationship, if you can get through some of the harder, tougher times, it can make relationships stronger. I'm talking about all relationships here, not just the relationship you have with your partner.

Each Relationship Is Unique

Relationship breakdown occurs when the health of the relationship isn't there. Just as we need to look after our own personal health, the health of a relationship needs to be taken just as seriously. This all comes back to being aware. As well as being self-aware, a couple needs to be aware of the relationship and its state. Now is the time to take stock of your relationship, and if it's not healthy, to sort out what is going on. Each relationship is unique. Health and happiness of individuals and the health and happiness of a couple is something that needs to be constantly worked on. Again, it comes down to personal awareness for each individual in the relationship. It's important not to take each other for granted.

Chapter 2 - Birds And The Bees

Harmony And Balance

Something that comes to mind when I'm talking about relationships is the word harmony. Slight changes are important in a relationship, especially a long-term one. Maintaining a healthy, long-term relationship with your partner requires a certain amount of skill. And this is where these are the wisdom years. Just as individuals can become wise in later years, a couple can become wise, too. It's about maintaining balance and harmony in a relationship.

Health With A Capital H

I have a great analogy for a healthy relationship. Think of the letter H. A capital H where the two sides are standing up straight and strong. In the middle, the bar that goes across the H stands for everything you have in common. Everything you've built up and worked towards. It could be a business or family, friends or a social group, hobbies, interests, property, mortgage, etc. The time you spend together, the activities you do together, the goals you have and your joint dreams. Everything is on that bar in the middle. All the while, each individual person (the upright parts of the letter H) is developing to their best ability. They concentrate on their own personal development, while the home, the family – the in-between part – is joint. It's an interest and it's a joint goal for both of you.

It Takes Two

An unhealthy relationship is more like a lowercase h, or even like the letter V. Let's look at the lowercase h first. One person is strong, confident and knows what they want as an individual. However, for the health of the relationship, if they're not aware of how the other person is feeling and if they don't put the work into the relationship, it doesn't stay a healthy one. The other side of the h is leaning over and trying to constantly support the partner. That other part of the h that's leaning over is actually suffering, because they're not developing themselves. They're constantly trying to ensure the relationship stays healthy.

Variables

Let's take the letter V. It's joined at the bottom. This is when you're both together. You've both got your goals and dreams. You start a life together, determined to build that future. If each individual starts growing strong and healthy that is good. However if each person grows in different directions, it's easy to grow apart over time instead of upwards together like the letter H.

Growing Upwards

Another way to describe a very healthy relationship is to think of that capital H, then extend it upwards like a ladder. This ladder represents two strong individual people growing together in a healthy way, improving and getting better. The sides of the ladder represent each person. The rungs of the ladder represent everything you're building together, such as the home you build together, your children, grandchildren and your mutual goals and dreams. It's important to develop interests together as you grow older and to maintain your physical and mental health individually as separate people. That capital H in the ladder represents a very healthy relationship.

The Main Game

So how do you keep your relationship healthy like that strong ladder? Firstly, keep your relationship as the main game. Treasure it and protect it. Be aware and work together with challenges that may arise. This includes challenges that happen in day-to-day life, such as financial, health and the usual bumps we encounter, as well as challengers, which

Chapter 2 - Birds And The Bees

can come in the form of toxic people or other influences. Keep yourself healthy as an individual, while also keeping the relationship healthy. If two people love each other, the relationship is worth working on. You need to keep that ladder solid and strong, which is achieved through your underlying love for each other and mutual respect. There needs to be good quality communication, and a sense of fun and playfulness. Seek assistance if you need it. Just as an individual wants to be the best person they can be, sometimes you may need some assistance with your relationship. Maintain your own physical and mental health and support each other with individual goals and dreams. This way you both lead a rich and fulfilled life both as individuals and as a couple.

Steps In The Ladder To A Good Strong, Healthy Relationship

- Each partner should spend time working on themselves so they can be the best they can be for themselves and for each other – couple development and personal development.
- Communicate honestly and openly. Express concerns. Say how you feel, what makes you feel that way, and express what you need from your partner. Your partner needs to be able to have his or her say also. It's important to really listen and take notice. I feel this is one of the most important steps.
- Share experiences, have fun together and create some wonderful memories.
- Grow together. Take care of each other. Practise self-care individually and as a couple.
- You can be the best that you can be together, as well as individually. You can also be a powerful positive force to make your world a better place for you and everyone who is in it.

Action Steps

1. Take responsibility for keeping healthy and have regular checks, such as pap smear tests and breast checks. Notice any signs of stress and seek assistance from a trusted professional.

2. Make a list of what you would like to do over the next five years and do it. Whether you are with a partner or single, you owe it to yourself to work towards fulfilling your goals and dreams. If in a relationship, you owe it to each other to share and strive to achieve your individual and mutual goals and dreams.

3. Pay attention to your language. What you say to yourself and what you and your partner say to each other. The first time you speak to someone in the morning – is it positive? Read up and find out about the five love languages. If you are single, this is a great quiz to take to learn more about yourself. Even if you have done this in your younger years, do the quiz again and see if anything has changed. As a couple, do the quiz so that you're aware of each other's love language. It's all about being aware of each other's needs and your own. This tool is even used in workplaces now as the language of appreciation.

Chapter 2 - Birds And The Bees

Resources

https://www.5lovelanguages.com/

Further reading and resource regarding PLOS Medicine Study from following source:
Mindbodygree.com – 2 August 2019 Article by Contributing Wellness Editor Stephanie Eckelkamp

3. Becoming

The Things We Learn

Isn't it funny how you remember some words for some unknown reason? My husband and I joke about a word I always remember. It's actually the official state fish of Hawaii, which is Humuhumunukunukuapua'a. It was years and years ago we went to Hawaii and I learned the name of that fish. I'm hoping to get that question in a trivia contest one day!

Another word stuck in my mind is the term 'bifurcation'. I learned this when I was doing my masters in NLP. Bifurcation is something that accompanies the onset of chaos. The *bifurcation point* is a point in space where you can expect to see a change in the behaviour of a system. During life, some of us reach that point where a change needs to be made. The famous baseball coach, Yogi Berra, said, "When you come to a fork in the road, take it", and this just about describes bifurcation.

The Fork In The Road

Different stages of our life can be preceded by an event or events that cause us to take a fork in the road. What is the alternative to taking that fork in the road? Camping out and being stuck in the one spot. Of course, major events can happen at any time. It may not even be a major event. It might be something that makes you decide to make a change in your life.

Choices

Life is made up of choices. Everyone has a choice. Even not making a choice is a choice in itself. Everything in life is a reflection of a choice you have made. If you want different results, you need to start making different choices. We don't always make the right choices. It's not about the mistakes you have made, but what you have learnt from those mistakes that defines you. If a mistake is made a second time, it's a conscious choice, not a mistake.

Change Is Good

Change is good. Sometimes change can come about from choices we've made. I think it's fascinating that our personalities evolve and change as we get older. Our personality is shaped by early life experiences and influences. Personality changes can also occur as a result of new life experiences. As we become older, our personality does slightly change.

Evolving

We're continuously developing. It's for this reason I've incorporated some coaching and some styling into this book. We are more than how we appear on the outside. Yes, we want to look the best we possibly can on the outside. We also want to be the best person we can be, and this comes from how we evolve as we get older. We never really stop changing and growing.

Chapter 3 - Becoming

Constant Curiosity

Think of your life as an exciting journey of discovery. As a coach, I maintain a constant sense of curiosity when dealing with my clients. This helps me ask the right questions so my client can take a look at their own life. Everything becomes crystal clear to them. It's all about being aware and learning about oneself.

Curiosity is an important ingredient to leading a successful, positive, ever-evolving life. It helps us learn about ourselves and other people. Curiosity can expand our empathy. Becoming more curious about yourself eliminates boredom. Become curious about yourself, your relationships and the possibilities for your life. Curiosity helps us gain knowledge about our constantly changing environment. Change is inevitable, so be curious about how you can best adapt to that change.

Awareness

Becoming self-aware is one of the best things you can do for yourself. If you take the awareness away from yourself and focus too much on what's going on around you, it's quite possible for you to lose touch with how you're feeling. Have you gone through a stage of getting dressed in the morning and realised you put your clothes on inside out?

This came as a sign to me all within one week. I was putting things on inside out. I was rushing out of the house without checking what shoes I was wearing. I had too many things on my mind and wasn't paying attention to myself and my own needs. As you can imagine, this is a good sign for a personal stylist that she has too much on her mind. Anyone who knows me knows that I love shoes. If I'm leaving the house wearing the wrong pair of shoes or not worrying about what's on my feet, that's a sure sign I'm not being self-aware!

Sometimes You Just Need To Stop And Rest

I first started to notice this when I attended a yoga retreat. I would get up in the morning at the retreat and keep putting my track suit jacket on inside out. It's really strange, but I knew this was a sign that I wasn't being self-aware. I was quite stressed before I attended the retreat. The meditation and yoga sessions helped me calm right down and I suddenly started to take notice of things like this. If I had kept going the way I was, I possibly could have been frustrated and kept getting more and more stressed. Being at the retreat made me stop and take notice. I became curious as to why this was happening. I realised I'd been doing other things too, such as not taking my key when leaving the apartment and being very absent-minded instead of mindful!

It's All Mindset

One of my coaching clients gave me some great feedback after 10 successful sessions. He had been able to make some huge identifiable changes. He said the best thing he gained from his sessions with me was self-awareness. He understood why he was behaving the way he was. It all comes back to what happens in our own mind. It's all to do with mindset.

Time and Space

When I was a consultant for a large organisation, I heard a great speaker say, "Leaders need time to think". This is true. Having time and space to think is when you become more self-aware. This is why meditation is so successful.

It's about letting go and not thinking about outside clutter that crowds your mind when you're trying to concentrate or focus on something. I've had to make time to focus on my writing and put everything else aside. I made it a priority because it was important to me.

Chapter 3 - Becoming

Stop And Look Within

We need to look within ourselves on a regular basis instead of waiting for something to happen to remind us to do this. It does tend to be when something drastic goes wrong that we stop and become more self-aware. At this time it's your opportunity to stop, take some notice of yourself. Develop that curiosity muscle and get interested in what is really going on for you.

Who You Become

> *"Watch your thoughts, they become words. Watch your words, they become actions. Watch your actions, they become habits. Watch your habits, they become character. Watch your character, it becomes your destiny."*
>
> **Lao Tzu, Chinese Philosopher**

Self-awareness is having a clear idea of who you are. It's knowing your personality, including your strengths, your weaknesses, your thoughts, your beliefs, your motivation and your emotions.

If you're not being self-aware, it means you're not paying attention to the most important thing you can do for yourself in your life. As a coach and as a stylist, I help people become more self-aware, or in other words, to really get to know themselves.

Multi-Tasking Is Not Effective

I now enjoy life so much. There are so many facets of my life I don't like to give up to concentrate on the other parts. I've tried to do everything at once and be superwoman. I've come to realise that multitasking just doesn't work. If there's one thing about myself I'd like to change, it would be to easily focus on one thing at a time. Multitasking is possible, but it isn't effective. It isn't something to be proud of. The brain can't effectively handle more than two complex related activities at the same time, and the thing you wish to change about yourself does require time and focus. This is my constant challenge.

Perfectly Imperfect

I joke and say that I'm a recovering perfectionist. I used to stop myself from doing things because I knew I would want it done perfectly. Because I coach myself and am self-aware, I have come to this realisation. I now make myself do things even though I realise it may not be perfect.

Striving For Excellence

Perfectionism is a personality trait which can lead to unhealthy obsessive conditions, such as OCD. Obsessive Compulsive Disorder needs professional help. Being self-aware helps you realise what you're good at, what you're not good at, what you like to do, what you don't like to do, how you like to look and how you don't like to look. It is all about knowing yourself. Being self-aware is healthy. Perfectionism is striving for flawlessness instead of simply being the best version of yourself and striving for excellence.

Focus On The Positives

Get to know what triggers you. Know what pushes your buttons. Then dig deeper and think, why am I like that? What is it? That is when that sense of curiosity comes in. Recognise your traits. Focus on your positive traits and those you can improve on. Know that it's completely okay to be perfectly imperfect.

Being Mindful

One of the ways you can become self-aware is mindfulness. Mindfulness comes about when you're focusing on one thing. By not worrying about the past or being concerned about the future, you focus on the present moment. You become more aware of your thoughts, your emotions, and how your physical body feels.

You'll notice your thoughts and your interpretations of life will begin to change. If you practise becoming more self-aware, it changes your mental state. It increases your emotional intelligence. This is really important in achieving what you want to in your life. My multitasking was sabotaging an ability to practise mindfulness.

Once you take notice and work out what it is that you want out of your life, you will realise you actually do have control. One of the positive side effects of becoming self-aware is that you also understand other people more. You become the master of your own future and relationships improve.

Something To Celebrate

At this stage of your life, you have the benefit of looking back on life's experiences and the result of what was achieved. This is something that doesn't happen as much when you are younger, and it's why I describe these years as the wisdom years. That's something to celebrate.

Better Than Yesterday

No matter what age you are or what stage you're at in your life, you can reflect on your day each evening. This way, you can constantly improve yourself. I believe that no one individual is better than another. We can each be better than we were yesterday.

Benefits Of Becoming More Self Aware

- Relationships improve. Your awareness increases about other people as well.
- You develop tools and strengths, especially in the area of discernment.
- You learn to cultivate relationships based on trust and respect.
- Communication with others improves.
- You understand how your emotions work and, in turn, understand and are more empathetic towards the emotions of others.
- By practising tools of self-reflection, you'll be able to look at decisions and choices you've made, noticing how you made them and what effect they had – whether or not those decisions or choices were the right ones for you.
- You look at decisions or choices you may have made involving other people, and whether your assumptions were correct or slightly misguided. This stops you from making mistakes again.
- You can admit mistakes if you find you were misguided or you made an incorrect assumption involving another person. This is a sign of strength, not weakness.
- Your credibility is improved when you admit these mistakes. It's when you ignore mistakes, stick your head in the sand or try to blame someone else that your credibility is damaged.
- You become even more self-aware by taking responsibility for your actions.
- Your health will improve. Self-awareness to do with health is paramount. You need to be aware of your body and how you're feeling, whether you're feeling fit or unfit, toned or need some exercise to work on your muscles. You need to be aware of how quickly you run out of breath. You need to be self-aware to notice if your heart is increasing in beats.
- Being self-aware helps you with your wardrobe and knowing what style suits you and what styles don't.
- No matter what age you are, it's never too late to change the aspects of yourself you may wish to change.

Chapter 3 - Becoming

Agent For Change

If you come to a fork in the road, look at where you're at. If you're getting the results you want, that's fine. Don't change that part. If you aren't getting the results, being self-aware enables you to take the other fork in the road and change whatever needs to be changed. Awareness is the greatest agent for change.

Action Steps

1. Get in the habit of increasing time for mindfulness. Take a walk in nature. My favourite place is the beach and it's a treat for me to get to there. I just absolutely love it. You can be mindful through meditation, going for walks, swimming... I love swimming. I used to swim laps in the swimming pool and repeat positive affirmations as I went. I find one of the best places to be mindful is when I'm on an airplane. There are no distractions, so I have the time to think and reflect.

2. Listen to yourself and your communication and really listen to other people. Don't just hear noise or someone talking, but really listen to what they're saying.

3. Journaling is something which is very powerful. If you have never done this before, I'd advise you start either in the morning or evening. Make it consistent. At times when you're feeling you just have too much on your plate or in your mind to become more self-aware or do any self-reflecting, just set aside some time to write whatever comes into your mind. It's called a 'Stream of Consciousness'. This is a practice that will really help you empty out and just leave your mind free for that self-awareness.

Resources

If you like guided meditations, try Calm, Headspace or Smiling Mind:

https://www.calm.com

https://www.headspace.com

https://www.smilingmind.com.au

4. Believing

Fill Your Cup

We only have one life. This is your life to live the best way you can. You're an amazing, beautiful, individual person, and by being the absolute best person you can be, you are powerful and in control of your own life. You can then be the best person for others as well. If your cup is overflowing, you've got so much more to give to other people. Believe in yourself and know you have all the resources inside you to be the best person you can be.

Blossom And Grow

I have some clients who are very special and have come a long way. One was a stay-at-home mum, who now has a thriving and expanding business doing what she loves, all because she believed in herself long before anyone else did. The style and confidence came from inside her. She just took the guidance provided and used it 100%. She continues to blossom and grow with confidence, as she now believes in herself and her own unique style.

Do you know what? Because she took that first step and believed in herself, others followed, and she is now an inspiration to them. You have the resources inside of you, too. You can shine and be an inspiration to yourself and others. You can maintain your confident style.

Reinforce Your Value

Keep a gratitude journal. Write about moments and people you're thankful for, and if you're feeling down, read that journal to lift your spirits. Reflect on the good. Give thanks for your blessings. List all the things that are great in your life – big, small and seemingly inconsequential. Do the things you enjoy. Often the activities you enjoy are the ones you most excel at. While engaging in these activities, you're also reinforcing how valuable you are. The more time you spend on sharpening your skills, the more your confidence will grow.

Your Unique Talents And Passions

Self-assessment is an important part of building your confidence. Looking at your own unique talents and passions and also determining where you want to improve, can help create action steps based on your findings. Self-knowledge results in a stronger and more confident you. Strengthen your strengths, identify your talents and build on them. Take advantage of what you do well to help you set and achieve your goals.

Design A Plan

Determine your passions and pursue them. What do you love to do? Spending your time pursuing your passions will refresh you. It will bring you another strength that you can depend on and more energy for all aspects of your life. Something which is really good to do is to write a 'me' speech. Give yourself permission to feel good about all your accomplishments. Every morning recite your speech, even if it's while going for a walk, or getting ready. Have a big smile on your face, even if you don't feel happy, as this helps create a happy mood.

Knowing Yourself

Be the best you can be and become better every day. It's all about knowing yourself and always being in tune with what works with you and your lifestyle. We never stop learning. There is more to you than where you live or what you wear. A lot of style is knowing yourself. It's about being healthy.

Knowing Your Style

Maintaining your style is not about always buying new clothes and having the latest fashion. It is more about making the most of what you have in your wardrobe. Keep learning about yourself and your style. Keep learning about what you like and what you don't like. Your likes and dislikes can change with age and circumstances. By practising self-awareness, you will be taking the time to know yourself. Over the years, outside influences can sometimes cloud your own opinions. I had one client tell me that after leaving a bad relationship she hadn't even know what colours she liked anymore.

Standing Tall

One of the best ways you can feel great, increase your confidence and keep your spine healthy, is to be conscious of always having the correct posture. If you have someone that can remind you, ask them to just give you a gentle nudge if you're slumping or slouching. This can happen when you are tired or spend a lot of time sitting and reading or working at a desk. If you spend a lot of time sitting, it's important to get up and get moving.

Pain In The Neck

If you use an iPad or a mobile phone, as many of us do, no matter what age you are, text neck can develop from constantly looking down. Keep your shoulders back and lifted when checking your phone by holding it closer to eye level.

Take plenty of breaks from looking at computer or iPad screens. Slouching and incorrect posture can lead to long-term back, shoulder and neck issues. Good posture has the power to help you avoid these problems, as well as improving your digestion, reducing stress and helping you gain even more confidence.

Heavy shoulder bags are the cause of a lot of issues with neck and shoulders. You'd be surprised at how carrying a bag on one side can actually make one shoulder lower than the other over the years. I now have one shoulder which is quite a bit lower than the other. I'm also aware that for years I would sit with one hip slightly tipped out when driving. I am determined to pass on this information in the hope it can help others.

It's All In The Doing/Activity

I've found that keeping an eye on my activity during the day does help. I've recently started doing Pilates three times a week, and if I don't, I suffer from sciatica. Yoga, walking, swimming and stretching is always going to be good for you. Remember to bring your shoulder blades down and then back, hold for two to three seconds and repeat this a few times each day.

Sleep On It

When it comes to sleeping, I personally have to remind myself not to sleep in the recovery position. It's probably one of the worst positions you can sleep in if you have back problems. Sleeping on your side or your back does help the spine to stay neutral. If you sleep on your side, remember to bring your legs up slightly and maybe place a pillow between your legs.

Take A Back Step

Another thing which is bad for you is high stiletto shoes. I'm a lover of high-heeled shoes, and I must admit, most of them I just keep to just look at now. The most comfortable shoes you can wear if you do like a heel are wedges. Stacked heels are also better than stilettos. No matter how much you love heels, it's good to have a break from them, because wearing heels can throw your weight forward and this is extremely bad for your back. You can still look sexy and sassy without super high heels.

Maintaining Your Health

Another way you can maintain your confidence is by looking after your body the best way you possibly can. No matter what number the scales say, it's all about how you feel personally. As far as losing weight goes, if you do need to, diet is only part of the equation. Health is all about balance and looking after your whole body. We're designed to move, so food and activity go hand in hand. Energy in and energy out. Each person is different. We often hear people say they want to go to the gym and get fit and toned. The most important part of exercise is that it needs to be consistent and easily maintained.

Exercise

Developing certain muscle groups is something a body builder may focus on. Every healthy person can maintain a good body shape by staying active and lifting weights relative to their lifestyle and physique.

We all have different physiques and it pays to work out what type of exercise suits you. Different body types benefit from different kinds of exercise. If you have any injuries or health issues, always check with your medical professional before starting anything new. Whatever you choose, make sure it's enjoyable for you, as this will make it easier to maintain.

Increase Endorphins And Confidence

Regular exercise increases the production of endorphins and confidence, which encourages you to make smart food choices. Leading a healthy lifestyle is all part of looking and feeling great. Nutrition is about feeding your body the fuel it needs to perform and regenerate healthy cells. So just like putting fuel into a car, your body won't run on empty. Also, filling your body with heavy unclean 'fuel' is going to make it sluggish and wear out a lot quicker.

Tips To Avoid Over-Eating

My tip is to balance your day and think about what you're about to eat. In other words, just stop and think. Ask yourself these questions: Am I thirsty? Am I bored? Am I tired? Am I emotionally empty? Am I eating out of habit? Am I curious as to how something tastes? Am I being polite? Have I put out enough energy today to balance out the calories I'll be putting in? Will I be active enough after eating to balance out the calories I'll be putting in? Is this very good for me, or is it just empty calories? Even an extra 400 calories a day over the recommended amount for your weight, height and energy expenditure, will put weight on over time. It's all a matter of thinking about what you're eating and thinking about what you're doing to balance everything else.

Chapter 4 - Believing

Stop And Do This

It's important to know how your body feels when you've eaten too much and how your it feels when you're eating a healthy amount for your height, frame and energy expenditure. Take notice of this and get used to what foods agree with you and what foods don't. My challenge to you is to put a note on the front screen of your phone or the refrigerator door, which says 'S-A-T', so you can remind yourself to stop and think. You can ask yourself those questions above. Grab yourself a drink of water each time you feel hungry if you know you have already eaten enough.

Many Reasons Now

We know so much more about ourselves and our bodies at this age, which means there are many reasons to feel more confident and have a healthier and higher self-esteem. There has been a lot of research, which shows that confidence in the majority of people does increase as you get older. It peaks when we pass the age of 50. When I asked a lot of people why they felt more confident in their 50s, most said they learned not to worry as much about what people think of them, and a lot claimed it's because they have greater self-awareness.

Influencers

There are many factors that affect self-confidence when we're younger. It could be childhood and the influences you are exposed to. It could be the pressure of society and what the media portrays. Friends and family can have a huge influence on a person's confidence. Relationships and the health of those relationships can have an impact on your confidence. When you're working, the environment you're in can affect your confidence. A major contributing factor is health. This is all the more reason to look after your health, to eat well, exercise and live a balanced life. Make sure your health team is supporting you in your journey. Find true professionals with your best interests at heart. Are they on a get well journey with you, or are they keeping you reliant on medications and dependant on them? Do you need to find better health professionals who can help you improve your overall health?

Only One Life

Abraham Maslow, an American psychologist, included self-esteem in his hierarchy of human needs. He described two different forms of esteem: the need for respect from others in the form of recognition, success and admiration, and the need for self-respect in the form of self-love, self-confidence, skill, or aptitude. Self-love plays an important part in having confidence. My advice is to find some things you're really good at and do them as much as you can. This is your time. This is your life. We only have one life and it's so important you spend it doing the things you love to do.

Impress Yourself!

At the age you are now, instead of trying to impress everyone else, how about each day seeking to impress yourself? Every time you do something you're happy with or that has been successful, say to yourself, "Well done". It could be something like mastering a new recipe, working out how to do something on the computer, or doing something you've always been afraid to do. Celebrate your wins no matter how small they may seem.

Believe in yourself and realise that to come this far in life, you have done so many wonderful things. You have set a good example for so many people. In the evenings look back at what you've achieved, no matter how big or small, and say to yourself, "I've impressed myself today and I appreciate myself".

Chapter 4 - Believing

Action Steps

1. Make a list of everything you have achieved in the last 12 months. Make sure you get everything down on paper. If you are stuck and can't think of anything (I am sure you can if you really put your mind to it) ask a friend or relative and they will help you get the ball rolling. Put the list somewhere you can see it.

2. Make a list of three things you really want to get done in the next 12 months. Goals you want to achieve. You can use the S.M.A.R.T system (Specific, Measurable, Achievable, Relevant and Time-based).

3. Know that you can achieve this goal because of the list you have in number 1 – if you have achieved once, you can achieve again. You just need to believe.

Resources

To find out your body type (Ectomorph, Mesomorph or Endomorph), and the type of exercise for each type, take this assessment. It only takes a few minutes and you don't need to sign up to anything:
https://www.bodybuilding.com/fun/becker3.htm

For a simple starter exercise at home (or anywhere) routine, download a program prepared by my friend Kaylene Gray from Tribe Fitness here:
http://bit.ly/AnywhereAnytimeWorkoutSheet

Further reading about S.M.A.R.T. Goals:
https://en.wikipedia.org/wiki/SMART_criteria

Find manufacturers and retailers of stylish comfortable shoes – one I have discovered recently is Scarlettos.com.au

Article on how to choose comfortable shoes:
http://beautyglow.com.au/why-buying-some-shoes-is-like-throwing-money-down-the-toilet/

5. Balancing Your Life

What does it mean to have balance in your life? People used to talk about work-life balance. Now, people keep working a lot later in life. They may start a business as they get older, or really enjoy their work. They may need to keep working longer for financial reasons. Personally, I don't believe that work-life balance is measured in hours or time that you spend working or not working. I believe it depends on how much time you spend doing what you love to do, and how much time you spend doing what you need to do.

All Or Nothing

It's all to do with the yin and the yang. Energy in and energy out. Spending and saving. Quiet times and busy times. Time alone and time with friends and family. Think of all areas of your life like a series of boxes: if you spend all your energy and time in one box and something happens to that one box, it leaves the rest of your life very, very empty, unloved, and uncared for.

Variety Is The Spice Of Life

There are plenty of reasons to have balance in your life. For one, it gives you variety so you don't become boring and your life doesn't become boring. You need to have a balance between what you need to do and what you want to do. Also, change is as good as a rest. If you're focusing on something and feeling frustrated, then having a rest from it will ensure you come back with renewed energy. One of my friends and I sometimes used to have what we called a "One Day Holiday" where we would fit in lots of things in one day that we wanted to do. We also used to meet on each Tuesday of the week and called it "Choose Day", where we would choose a place to go for a long walk to and go for lunch or a coffee. We explored different areas of the city and tried new cafes.

Tipping Those Scales

Having a balance between busy times and quiet times keeps you calm and grounded. It keeps you ready and energetic when you need motivation. If you are caring for others in your life, you need to keep a balance, because if you care too much for others and forget to care for yourself, your health can suffer. For myself, as a Libran with my star sign being the scales, it really does make a difference. Balance is very important to me and I can feel when things are out of balance.

We need to keep the physical and emotional side of our life balanced, as well as the spiritual side. The physical side includes health, rest and exercise. It means healthy eating, while also giving yourself the occasional treat. I don't believe in depriving yourself of the things you love. On the other side of the scales, stay aware of how much you are indulging in things that aren't good for you.

Chapter 5 - Balancing Your Life

Quality Time

Emotional balance is important, too. You need to keep a track of how much time you spend with family and how much time you spend with friends. Although you get pleasure from being with these people, it's also important you spend some quality time with yourself. There needs to be a balance between fun times and relaxation time.

Inside And Outside

If you're someone who likes to focus on the external, including helping others and charity work, as well as outside interests, such as building a business and sports activities, it's really good to balance that time with looking after yourself. Overwork can be damaging to your own health by not paying attention to your heart and mind. This can lead to high levels of stress. Take time to focus on the internal as well.

Home And Away

Even when you come back from a holiday, it's a relief to get back to the everyday activities of cooking meals, looking after your house and your normal routine.

Toned And Tough

You need to have a balance with exercise. If you're doing a lot of weight training or weight bearing exercise, you need to balance this with some stretching and cardiovascular exercise.

Wheel Of Life

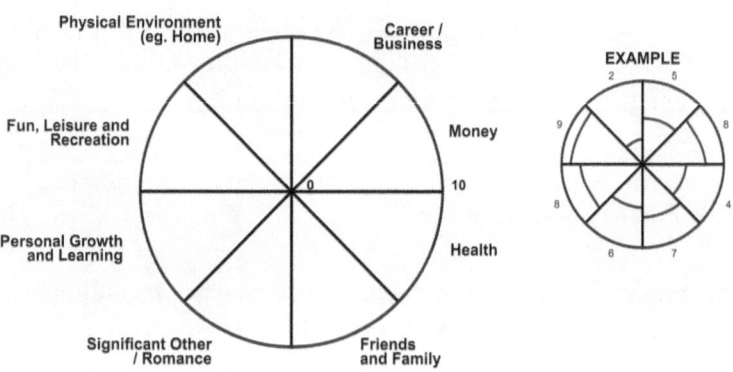

One of the best ways to determine how much balance you have in your life is to look at something called the Wheel of Life. Each of these segments determines how much time you are spending in this area. The centre of the wheel is a 0, the outside of the wheel signifies a 10. Look at things like your business or your career, or if you're retired add in looking after your home or just general day-to-day running of your life.

Take some quiet time to look at this and think about each area on the wheel. Ask yourself each question to do with that particular area of your life. This is a valuable exercise to go through. There is a link at the end of this chapter to obtain a resource to assist.

Study And Learning

Look at your goals in this area. Have a think about whether you are satisfied or dissatisfied with it. If you're not satisfied with it, start it at zero and mark it out of 10. For example, if you are absolutely not learning anything new at the moment it may be a 0 or a 1.

Chapter 5 - Balancing Your Life

Work And Business

If you have a business, look at your growth plan for it. Look at the number of customers or clients you have. Look at the lifestyle you're experiencing because of your business. Is it what you want? Give it a mark out of 10.

Money, Money, Money

Look at your finances. Are you happy with where you are at? Do you have a passive income, or would you like to have one? Are you happy with the total outgoings you have? Are you happy with the amount of savings you have? Are you happy with your financial stability at the moment? Do you have investments? Do you have any long-term financial plans? Do you have some money put aside for your next holiday? Do you have a few bank accounts and are they all satisfying your needs? Are you paying too much in bank fees or is it worthwhile looking to see if you can change anything? Mark this a score out of 10.

Health Is Your Wealth

Look at your health. How healthy do you feel? Are you eating the right sort of foods? Are you getting the right sort of exercise? Are you drinking enough water and do you have enough relaxation time? What about your sleep? Do you get enough at night? How do you feel in terms of your daily vitality? How often do you get sick with colds and flus and anything else that's going around? Are you dealing with any long-term or chronic illnesses?

Have a look at your health in general. Are you fit and do you have plenty of energy? Do you smoke or drink too much? Is your weight within the healthy range? Give it a score out of 10.

Family And Friends

Have a look at the time you spend with family and friends. Do you see them enough, too much, or just the right amount? The quality of relationships with these people, the people that you care for, are really important. Are there any conversations you need to have? Any tensions? Anything left unsaid between you? Any 'elephants in the room' that have been left to fester.

It's been said that we have friends for a reason, a season, or a lifetime. I know that I have some very special friends. Some friends I don't see very often. When I see them again we pick up as though we've never had that space away from each other.

With regard to these relationships, if you can see a positive future and if things are good, that's great. If things are on a downhill slide, there's no need to keep anyone in your world or in your life who you don't need to have in there. It's really important to have positive relationships with everyone in your life. Take it all into account and give family and friends a score out of 10. You could even split the segment in two.

Romance

Look at the romance in your life. Do you have some time out with your significant other? Look at the quality of time you spend with your partner. Do you have feelings of love and appreciation? Do you have a sense of satisfaction with your relationship? Do you have the emotional and physical connection you need and is your partner meeting your love language?

If you don't have a significant other, you can look at the romance and the love you have for yourself. Do you have an appreciation for yourself? Do give yourself quality time? Do you have that emotional connection you need to have with yourself? Take a look at this as well and mark out of 10.

Chapter 5 - Balancing Your Life

Personal Growth

Have a look at personal growth on your Wheel of Life. Do you feel you're growing and learning every day? How is your emotional growth? Your intellectual growth? It could be something like dealing with any emotional baggage you may have hanging around. Getting past those old blockages and getting rid of behaviours that no longer serve you is important. Are you aware of who you are and what brings you to the sense of self? Can you say to yourself. "This is me, this is who I really am". Take a look and give it a mark out of 10.

Playtime

Have a look at your fun and recreation. How much time do you spend having fun? Do you spend time with friends just laughing and having a good time? Do you have a good balance? Are you doing quality things that really satisfy you? Are they what you would call high-quality activities? How often do you make time for fun and recreation? Are you enjoying your free time, or are you doing activities that aren't enjoyable and just going through the motions? Life is full of ups and downs and fun times are important to slot into your Wheel of Life. Mark this section out of 10.

Are you getting a good sense of adventure? Do you have a social connection with other people? Using fun and recreation to help you grow personally is important. Is this contributing to all your other goals? Is it ecological? Are you eating out instead of doing sports or exercising? Then this part could be affecting your health goal. If you're feeling that you're overweight and finding that you're eating out more than exercising, you need to look at this. I meet a friend for a walk every week and I find this way I'm combining some quality social time with some exercise. Take all this into account and mark it out of 10.

Environment

Have a look at your physical environment. Are you comfortable where you're living? Are you happy with your home? Would you like to tweak and adjust it and maybe redecorate in some way? Do you have enough space? Do you have too much space? Are you surrounded by your perfect environment, whether it's beautiful and sophisticated or natural, in the city or in the country? Do you have easy access to public transport or driving? Do you have enough fresh air? Do you have enough natural light? If it's an apartment, is it easy to get to? Do you have too many stairs? Take into account everything about your current living situation and give it a score from 0 to 10.

Changes

For each of these parts of your life which make up the wheel, think about how you currently spend your time. Think about how you would like to spend time in this area. Write down any changes you'd like to see. Can you make these changes yourself, or do you need someone else to help? For example, if it's health and fitness you'd like some help with, maybe you could see a personal trainer or take up an exercise class.

For each section, work out what actions, choices or decisions you could take or make that would bring it to a 10 out of 10 for you. Just imagine how a 10 out of 10 would feel for each of these sections. Just as a wonky lopsided bicycle wheel or a car wheel is going to be very clunky and uncomfortable to ride on, so is your life if it isn't balanced. If any of these areas in your wheel is very low, then take a look at it and see how you can balance your life more.

Constant Adjustments

This is going to be a constant process, because life happens. It's not something that's going to be fixed in one week. The main thing is to enjoy what you're doing and make the most out of your life. Treasure every day.

New Opportunity

Now is a new stage of opportunity. It's an opportunity to work on those areas you may not have been able to work on before. It's really important to always look at the present and not too much in the past. This is why looking at the Wheel of Life is very valuable, as it keeps you in the present. Balance in life is the answer.

Effortless Balance

If you spend too much of your life in one area, the other areas get neglected. Sometimes we only realise this when we get to older years. Balance can be effortless. You will know when you're leading a very balanced life, because you will feel calm. You will also feel excited when it's time to feel excited. It's like you have this sense of absolute peace and joy.

No Room For Stress

I know in past years when I've had a lot of stress in my life, I've felt an inner turmoil. It was constant and it was always there. Stress can do dreadful things to people. During my coaching studies, I have learnt about the effect stress can have on people. It can change personalities and ruin relationships. If you have balance in your life, there is no room for unhealthy stress. If you have balance in your life, when things crop up, like too much work or drama, you can deal with it. You're keeping your connections and relationships strong. Your personal development has been worked on. You're aware of where everything sits in that scale, on that Wheel of Life.

Paying Attention

This is how important self-awareness is. When you're self-aware, you realise when things are out of balance. This book is about the inside as much as it is about the outside of each woman. Pay attention to your emotional health, your spiritual health, and how you feel. Your confidence will be affected if you're only thinking about the outside image. That is not living a sassy and stylish life.

Where Is The Sass?

You may be stylish, but where's the rest? The sass comes from being self-aware, and self-sufficient. Self-sufficient doesn't mean you don't need other people. By being self-aware and self-sufficient, you understand yourself and what you need. If you need help, reach out and ask for it. Being self-sufficient, stylish, having great interaction with others and leading a good life, are some of the things that contribute to that well-balanced Wheel of Life.

Visualise And Feel

Doing exercises, such as looking at the Wheel of Life, gives you a sense of satisfaction. You now know the importance of being self-aware. You can look at this and just know what you need to do to balance your life. You can visualise and feel – close your eyes, see what you see, feel what you feel, hear what you hear…what would it be like to have a 10 in these areas? Then take small steps to live the way you want and improve on these sections. Once you've looked at these needs and realised what they are, you can clearly define them and express them. It's a matter of taking responsibility and fulfilling your needs.

Chapter 5 - Balancing Your Life

Taking Responsibility

Even expressing a need to someone else is being self-sufficient, because you're taking steps. You're taking responsibility to express what it is you need. Leading a balanced and well-formed life – a nice smooth circle of life, which will get a bit wobbly from time to time – is key to a good life. Part of the answer is taking responsibility and doing something about it to sort out the wobbly bits of the wheel. The goal is balance.

Action Steps

1. Go online and print off your copy of the Wheel of Life from the link below. Complete it as above. Date the top of the sheet and on the back write notes of the steps you need to take to even out those segments. Do you need someone or something to help you achieve a higher score for those segments? Make note of this also.

2. In a month, print off another copy and see how much each segment has improved. Repeat what you did above.

3. Do this again in month 3 and take notice if the wheel has evened out or if there are areas you need to work harder on. These constant adjustments keep everything in balance.

Resources

Wheel of Life document:
Wheel of Life document to print link below:
www.bstyledforlife.com.au/resources
Password is Style50

Part 2
THE OUTSIDE

6. Booties, Boobies and other Bits

What is a definition of looking good? It's balance and symmetry.

> *"Women try to force their figures into fads and trends even if they're not flattering to them because they think they're sexy – but it's really all about balancing the body."*
>
> **– Bradley Bayou,
> Fashion Designer & Author 'The Science of Sexy'**

No Body Is Perfect

We've looked at life balance and now we'll go into physical balance – the body. The human body is amazing. I've always been fascinated by the human body's ability to perform everything it does. Two amazing experiences have been attending University Wet Lab at St Lucia while studying Anatomy and Physiology for my Beauty Therapy Diploma, and going to the Body Worlds Exposition in London. When looking at the human body objectively (as you really need to at these two places), you can see there is no right or wrong, or perfect body. We are all a collection of body parts – head, neck, torso, arms and legs.

When I see a client for a styling appointment, the only time I use a tape measure is when I'm advising how to alter a garment, such as how many centimetres to take a hem or a sleeve up. No measuring the actual client. This is how I was trained and I like that it's purely visual and not at all invasive for the client.

Beautiful Unique Architecture

If we think of a body shape like a building, the architecture is varied and unique to each person. The outside structure, or architecture of the body, is the silhouette or external shape of the body. There are certain garments that look best on certain body shapes. You might be bigger in the bottom, top or middle areas. You could have straight lines, or you could be curvy. You may be proportionally balanced on the top and bottom. You could have a longer torso than legs or be longer in the legs than the torso.

Personal styling is just that – it's personal. As I have shared in previous chapters, the key is getting to know yourself. Having your own personal style comes from within. How you dress and accessorise is all part of that styling. As well as 'Style Personality' and likes and dislikes, there's how to wear clothing and accessories to best suit our huge variety of body shapes and sizes.

All The Bits And Bobs

I am speaking objectively about the different shapes and proportions of the human body and how the eye perceives those variations. Body variations are factors, such as bust, stomach and ankle size. All the bits and bobs we have, which vary and change as we get older.

Once you know your body shape, your body proportions and your body variations, it's so much easier to choose clothes that are going to suit you.

Chapter 6 - Booties, Boobies And Other Bits

Body proportions are length of areas, such as torso and legs. You can have a long torso and short legs, a short torso and long legs or balanced torso and legs.

Body variations are the parts of your body that vary from person to person. You may have a large or a small bust, large or flat backside or "booty", or larger arms that you may want to take attention away from. Our neck length and décolletage area can also vary. You can dress to highlight or to minimise these areas.

Body shapes X, H, A, V, I, O, 8. My clients come to me because they want to know the right clothing to wear for their body shape. I'm going to cover these seven main body shapes.

X Shape

The first body shape is the X. Some stylists or image consultants will call this the hourglass. The X shape is very feminine and curvy, often with a large bust, slim waist and curvy hips. The X and 8 shapes are quite similar. You have a slow curve that starts above the waistline and goes down to the lower hip line. It's good to wear clothes that are well-fitting without being too tight. With the X shape, simplicity is the key. Look for clean, simple tops with scoop neck lines. Three-quarter sleeves are really good. These can make you look taller. Avoid too much layering and look for belts that help define the waist.

You look best in princess seams and long, shapely seams that gather at the waist and flare out again at the hips. Go for a smooth, snug look and show off your contours. Well-tailored and fitted jackets, maybe with a peplum or a little flare out after the waistline, are going to look great on you. Avoid things like the Chanel type jacket, which is too boxy looking. I have purchased jackets like this because I loved the fabric and pattern and had them shaped in at the waist. They now look great. With the bottoms, you're going to look best in skirts that stop at or below the knee, but preferably not above it. Pencil skirts are going to look really good on you. Choose pencil skirts that follow your natural curve and go with fitted options, but not too tight. Bootleg pants and skinny jeans also look good on you.

It's good to keep it simple with solid colours. Prints can actually disguise your figure, rather than highlight it. It all depends on which areas of your body you want to highlight. Avoid a lot of extra fabric. Have some stretch in the fabric as opposed to any fabrics that are too stiff and starchy. Think about following the curves of your body and some draping in areas that you don't want to have too much cling. Colour looks great on your body type, as do monochromatic outfits.

H Shape

The H body shape goes straight up and down and the waistline doesn't go in much. Keep details above the bust or along the hemline and away from your middle area. If you choose to wear belts, make sure they are quite simple in style. Adding anything in a light colour around the waist will only make this area look heavier and even more undefined. Stiff and shapeless garments will only emphasise your rectangle shape.

Chapter 6 - Booties, Boobies And Other Bits

Empire waistlines, or anything high waisted, is great for the H Shape. Scoop necklines, sweetheart necklines and basically anything with detail around the neck is good as it draws the attention upwards. If you're large busted, scoop necks are more flattering. With the bottom half, you can wear all sorts of pants and jeans, from skinny or slim legs to wide legs and anything flowing or draping. This will look feminine for your frame and will really soften that H body shape.

A good tip is to make sure your jeans and pants are fitted around your hips and thighs to help to create curves. Most skirt styles are going to look great on you, along with anything with frills and layers, as long as it's not too full and voluminous. Prints will look feminine and flattering on your shape. Button-down shirts draw the attention vertically down the middle of your body. This divides the body in half vertically which can make the waist area look narrower. Shoes are a great asset. If you're a shoe lover – there you go! Great reason to buy shoes. The main thing to remember is you want to keep the interest high or low on your body and draw attention away from the middle.

A Shape

For the A body shape, your best features are your legs. You've got narrow shoulders and wider hips, so you want to give your body real feminine appeal. Your instinct might be to show off your slender upper body. Resist this, because tiny tops throw off your body's balance, making the lower part look bigger than it actually is. The idea is to concentrate on putting the detail on top and to think about layers. Creating balance for your shape is all about filling up your upper half especially around the shoulder area. Cardigans are great for A shapes, because they add lightweight volume. In colder weather, try cropped jackets that stop at the waist. You are a body type that can wear the Chanel type jackets that Jackie Onassis used to wear.

Don't be afraid to show a little skin. Three-quarter sleeves, wide scoop necks and one-shoulder tops all look fabulous on you. Boot-cut pants are also great and the slight flare helps to balance out curve, especially if you wear them with a heel. This will give your legs a little bit more length. You can wear straight leg pants and jeans also. Avoid pants that are too loose or that have skinny legs. Go for dark coloured, medium-rise jeans with simple stitching and pockets in the back. For skirts and dresses, try

Chapter 6 - Booties, Boobies And Other Bits

a classic A-line cut that falls softly over your curves and highlights your waist. Avoid high-waisted and pleated skirts, they are better for people who have a more straight up and down type figure.

Draw the eye upwards with bright-coloured, embellished tops. Try a boat neck shirt with horizontal stripes, or a cardigan with a rosette or a broach. Chunky jewellery can look great on you too, because it adds interest up top. This is where you want to add the bulk and the attention. Prints and patterns are fine for your lower body, but aim for darker colours on the bottom and lighter colours up top. Another tip is to use short sleeves to add width to the top area.

V Shape

The V body shape is like a swimmer's body shape. You've got a tapered torso, a smaller waist and great legs. This can make you look confident and fit. Your legs are normally well sculpted, so your instinct might be to show them off with leggings. This works if you're wearing a long top below your back side, but in general you want to add volume to your lower half, not your top half. You look great in cowl necks and deep Vs, which help to minimise the strong upper body you've got. Go for simple, fuss-free shirts without ruffles and add some feminine looks to your tops. Halter necks because of the V shape (upside-down) is a good style because the diagonal lines draw the eye up to the neck. Use fabric that gently drapes over your body. Anything with movement and softness, such as flutter-type sleeves, is good. Avoid wearing thin straps as they will make your shoulders look broader.

Amplify your lower half to match the fullness of your upper body. Wide leg pants or long skirts create balance. This depends on your height – they can actually make you look shorter if you're under about five foot four. As a general rule, look for anything that's flowing. Go for full-bodied pants and skirts, which make your body look bigger.

Have fun with embellished shoes to call attention to your feet. Keep jewellery minimal on top, but get creative with bangles and rings to accessorise your outfits. Use light colours and prints below the belt to draw the attention to the lower half of the body. Stick to darker colours on top as this creates more balance. Carry larger purses at your side or in the bend of your arm to avoid adding volume on top. It does depend on where you carry your bag. If you're carrying a shoulder bag and it's large, that's going to add more volume.

O Shape

The Beautiful O body shape. Your best features are that you look feminine and soft. The common pitfall with the O body shape, is trying to cover up your body. You can show off your neckline, your forearms and your great legs. Your goal is to add structure to your

Chapter 6 - Booties, Boobies And Other Bits

body, especially on top. Try a structured jacket like a blazer and have angles and lines across your body with wrap dresses or asymmetrical hemlines. These are great because they confuse the eye. Draped fabrics, cowl necks and flutter sleeves look great on you, too.

You can keep everything looking feminine and still have structure to your fabric. You can layer with dressy tank tops that have a bit of Lycra or stretch to them. A slim line, straight leg or boot cut is going to be great for you when you're wearing trousers. Wearing high heels takes off some weight and shows off your legs. Dresses with ruching or gathering hide your tummy and create an hourglass fit, as long as it's subtle without too much detail or fabric. Patterns and prints look great on you, especially on your upper body. Floral or geometrical prints are great. Irregular patterns are best as they're more slimming. Stick to fabrics with a bit of weight to them, like the heavy cottons or muslin. Material that's got a bit more of a natural structure.

I Shape

The I body shape is the model's body shape. They can wear any type of clothing and this is what designers use to show off their new designs. With the I body shape, your goal is to add some feminine shape to your clothing and some detail at the waistline.

Wear fabric with a little bit of weight and volume to it and add some feminine detail. Try to avoid clothes that are too sparse. You can get away with lots of fabric, so get adventurous with what you're wearing. You can wear a lot of the latest designs that are shown in including layers and frills.

Chapter 6 - Booties, Boobies And Other Bits

Benefits Of Knowing Your Body Shape

The fun part is you can dress according to your body shape to create a variety of outfits. This is not about being perfect. It's about knowing what you like and knowing what's going to look good on you. This will make you feel great and give you even more confidence.

The other benefit is that you're going to feel both psychologically and physically comfortable in your clothes.

Body Proportions

One of the main places you will see the importance of body proportions is when you go to a jeans shop. Have you seen the huge variety of jeans that you can buy nowadays? High-rise, mid-rise, low-rise and bottom shaper. This is even before you get to the denim colour, stitching colour, washed, over-dyed, boot cut, straight leg, slim line, skinny leg, boyfriend jeans, ripped jeans, patched jeans, distressed jeans, and the list goes on and on. The good part about knowing your genetic body proportions is you can change your look by what you wear.

You get to know what to wear and what not to wear. If you have short legs, wearing a long cardigan down past the knees will make your legs look shorter. Someone with a long torso wearing a low-slung belt around the hips accentuates the length of the torso. It's quite often not until you see a photograph of yourself that you realise how important it is to understand body proportions and what to wear.

Variety of Lengths, Widths, Sizes

Body variations is the other part of the equation. Everybody's different and we all have body variations. This is what makes us so interesting. It would be awful if we were all clones of each other – we'd be like plastic dolls. We are all different sizes, with different limb lengths, different-sized body parts and different shapes. Wherever we put the detail and emphasis is where the attention will go to. There are so many tips and tricks to visually adjust your body proportions and body variations, as well as body shape.

Tips And Tricks

The larger the print, the larger it will make you look. Muted prints are more slimming than bright prints, and regular repeating patterns aren't as slimming as random patterns. Heavy arms can be covered up with sheer sleeves that don't bulk. Short necks can be made to look longer with a lower neckline. If you've got heavy thighs and ankles, these can be distracted from as well. Remember that any area you want to distract from keep plain and undetailed. Darker colours recede and lighter brighter colours advance (get noticed first). The small bust, long necks, strong thighs and protruding tummy can all be disguised. Boot leg pants and jeans are great for balancing. If you have short legs and a long torso, knee-length skirts are best. If you have a short mid body, keep the detail away from it.

Models And Movie Stars

Now that you've figured out your body shape, your body proportions and body variations, you'll know where to add the detail and interest to your outfits and where to keep it plain and simple. Most people aren't happy with their body shape or proportions. Everyone on this planet – even models and movie stars – find something they don't like about their body. This is completely normal. It's something we all need to address – to be kinder to ourselves and less critical. Not knowing your body shape or body proportions means you can exaggerate any areas of your body that may be out of proportion or you may not be happy with. This is all to make you feel better and to assist you to get creative with your style.

Chapter 6 - Booties, Boobies And Other Bits

Some people may find they're a combination of two body shapes. You may have an upper body shape that varies from your lower body shape. This is when you would dress according to what suits each part of the body. The important thing is to be happy with what you have and make the most of your genetic assets.

Be happy and healthy – look good and feel good and vice versa. That is the way it works.

Action Steps

1. Take an objective look at photographs of yourself. The key here is objective, not critical.

2. Take notice of which photographs you look best in and what you are wearing.

3. You can download a body proportion chart (link in Resources).

4. Find out if you are short waisted or long waisted by tipping to the side (like a teapot) – put your hand in the middle of that curve. This is your waist area. If you can fit two hands sideways above your waistline and up to your bustline you have a balanced waist. If you can fit more than two hands, then you are long waisted, and if you can only fit one-and-a-half hands between your bustline and your waist, then you are short waisted.

Chapter 6 - Booties, Boobies And Other Bits

Resources

If you are unsure what body shape you are a calculator can be downloaded from the link below:
www.bstyledforlife.com.au/resources
Password is Style50

7.
Being You

"Style is a way to say who you are without having to speak."

- Rachel Zoe

The best person to look like when you get dressed is yourself. Even if you have someone you'd like to model yourself on, you are the best and most authentic version of yourself. I'm going to outline some of the style personalities I use when image consulting. See if you can recognise yourself as one of these. Your style personality is something that can change over the years. For example, if you were a rebellious style personality and used to wear lots of studs and zips, with some piercings and tattoos, you may have mellowed and changed as you got a little bit older.

Congruency Is Comfortable

Style personality is something that's really important, because you need to feel congruent. You need to look the way you feel inside. I'm a great believer in showing your personality on the outside. For example, can you imagine how someone with a soft, feminine personality, would feel if she was told to walk out of the house wearing a pair of high-heeled, patent black stilettos with a black leather biker jacket, a very, very tight fitting skirt, a revealing low-cut shiny blouse, a whole lot of rings on her fingers and a bag that was very large and chunky?

Just the same way a person who likes to make a big impact when they walk into a room would feel if they were told that they needed to wear a dress that was a very demure, classic style, and some low-heeled shoes and a neutral colour scheme to blend into the background. It would really affect her personality – and in a not good way!

Style Personalities Can Change

This can change with lifestyle, age and circumstances. For example, if someone is a dramatic style personality and wears quite striking, firm, synthetic fabrics, which are slim fitted and tailored and moved countries to a very hot climate, they need to adapt their style personality to incorporate more natural fabrics. They would not want to wear the jackets they used to and might become more relaxed in their style. Likewise, someone who used to work in a corporate environment may now have the opportunity to wear the clothing they really love if they are a naturally relaxed style. It's important that you work out what clothing you like to wear.

Benefits

There are many benefits to knowing what your style personality is:

- ✓ You look congruent with your personality.
- ✓ Great for branding if you're in business.
- ✓ Everything goes with everything. Simplify your wardrobe.
- ✓ Easy packing to go away – everything co-ordinates.
- ✓ You get to know what types of shops carry your style.

Chapter 7 - Being You

- ✓ Friends and family will find it easier to buy you gifts .
- ✓ People can let you know if they see 'your style' somewhere.

What a great compliment to receive when someone says, "I saw this dress the other day and it was so you".

When I conduct a style consultation, I do a Style Personality Assessment, and find that some women are a combination of two different style personalities. One will be more dominant than the other.

I'm going to go through the different style personalities. See if you can recognise yourself in one of the following descriptions.

Classic

The classic woman is all about keeping garments nice and simple. She likes to look conservative, but also relatively up to date. She always maintains her clothing and makes sure it doesn't date too quickly.

Everything will look elegantly styled. She has a styled haircut, perhaps in a bob, or if it's shorter it will be an easy-to-maintain style and will always be kept trimmed. Even if it's shoulder length or longer, it will be well maintained, possibly in a ponytail or up style. She wears trousers or skirts, usually in plain colours, and teams these with a shirt or blazer. If she does wear patterns, some of her favourite combinations may be stripes, polka dots, herringbone, or small prints.

Relaxed/Natural

This style personality is all about comfort. She doesn't want to wear anything that's uncomfortable or restrictive. She likes to look feminine, while staying comfortable. She doesn't normally wear a lot of makeup, and her hair is in a no-fuss style, for example, tied back in a ponytail.

Chapter 7 - Being You

She will look after her hair, but will make sure it's easy to look after without much product. Makeup is very minimal, with maybe a little bit of lip gloss and some mascara.

The relaxed style personality wears fabric that is normally quite natural, such as cottons or linen. She loves to wear anything that's stretchy and comfortable. Capri pants and track suits are popular choices. She is usually active and ready to go and just do what needs to be done. She loves natural colours: greens, blues, browns, anything you would find in nature. She loves to wear texture and it must feel nice as well. The relaxed style personality needs to be able to move, and she likes to wear layers so she doesn't have to change during the day.

If she's wearing jackets, they're normally quite soft and drapey. If she could wear joggers or runners all the time, she would. She always prefers low heels and likes to wear underwear made from natural fabrics with smooth finishes. Jewellery could be anything that's made from nature, possibly wooden earrings, wooden necklaces, and her watch will normally be quite simple and functional. She loves wooden-framed sunglasses and won't wear anything that's really shiny or glitzy. The relaxed style personality loves to use a backpack as a handbag, or a large shoulder bag. She will wear anything that's made from leather, suede or material. She's not fussy with what accessories she uses, for example a pen will just be any pen she can find.

Dramatic

The dramatic style personality is someone who likes to make an impact when they walk into a room. She loves fabric patterns, such as animal or geometric prints, and anything with a shine or sheen. Dramatics prefer large-scale prints to smaller ones. She loves bright, vibrant colours, such as hot pinks, bright blues and reds. Her lipstick will be quite bright and bold. Her hair will be quite structured. If she has short hair, it will be a precision haircut, which needs to be maintained every three or four weeks. She won't have any hair out of place. Her grooming is impeccable. She would prefer to be wearing the latest designer fashion outfit over anything that's just off the rack and on sale.

Dramatics like to have simple, edgy designs to their clothing. Anything with a contrast appeals to them, such as fur vests and fur jackets, possibly combined with leather pants and skirts. The dramatic style personality loves to have a cinched-in waist and big collars with sharp angles on them. She loves stiletto shoes and is happiest in anything that's a little bit different and 'out there'. She likes to have glitzy trims on accessories, such as shoes and handbags.

She likes to wear jewellery that really stands out, such as a statement necklace or ring. Her glasses or sunglasses will be very straight and angular, and are likely to be red or a bit different. Dramatics won't wear anything that's soft looking. The dramatic style personality loves a patent handbag or something that's very different and creates a statement. She doesn't mind wearing brand names and is keen to have the latest fashion.

Creative

The creative style personality loves to wear clothes they've made, designed or altered themselves. It could be florals with stripes, or stripes and spots. She isn't too fussy about the type of fabric and enjoys clashing colours. The creative style personality really loves to show her personality on the outside, by wearing anything that's original. She isn't going to risk looking like someone else when they go to an event. She might be a bit hippy or arty looking, or very out there with geometrical colours. The creative style personality is similar to the dramatic, but she doesn't mind wearing more subtle colours. She shows everyone she has a creative side to her personality.

The creatives like to wear fun underwear, such as bright colours, and to mix and match patterns. Her jewellery won't be bought from a traditional jewellery store, and will be quite funky and arty. Her watch will be a bit unusual. Her glasses will asymmetrical. A favourite style is retro, especially when it comes to handbags and accessories. She will use something that shows how creative she is, such as a shopping bag she obtained overseas and had altered in some way, or that she has dyed. It could be a cute little suitcase-style bag – anything fun.

Rebellious

The rebellious style personality is just that. They like to rebel. She won't be predictable and likes to make a statement. She likes to show she can do whatever she wants. In younger years, she may wear something with lots of studs, skulls and crossbones. She may have a lot of tattoos, and as she gets older, possibly still likes a lot of these 'Ed Harry' types of designs. Anything with spiderwebs, lace, leather and denim, big chunky necklaces and chains. She loves black and anything that's dark and quite bold looking.

She likes to wear things that are big in design and can be shiny or matte. Quite often she'll have piercings. She loves to wear tights with Doc Marten or biker boots. She will quite often wear stilettos. She likes to wear jeans and graphic design T-shirts. She loves to wear anything with a lot of detailing, such as zips, buttons. and studs. She loves underwear that's sexy and lacy, possibly push-up bras, and anything that's black. She loves to wear safety-pin type jewellery, or anything that's big, shiny and chains. She normally goes for metal or plastic framed glasses. Quite often she'll wear cat eye frames, or really oversized sunglasses, just to give that sense of rebellion. The rebellious style personality likes to use a small novelty handbag, with lots of studs and zips on her bag.

Feminine Romantic

The feminine or romantic style personality loves soft florals, small prints and flowing fabrics. She is the complete opposite to the rebellious style personality. She loves anything that's rounded and curved. She loves the feel of soft fabric against her skin. She loves soft pink nail polish, or a French manicure. Her makeup and hair will be soft. Even if it's short hair, it won't be in a severe or harsh precision cut.

The feminine style personality can be quite tricky as she gets older. She loves long, curly hair styles and needs to ensure the hairstyle doesn't look too young and girlish. She loves to wear cardigans and have beautiful fabrics in her wardrobe. She loves pastel colours, with soft blues, soft pinks, mauves, apricots, and will be quite careful to make sure she always look feminine. She loves fabrics that are soft to touch, like velvet and silk. She loves soft cottons. Everything has a soft finish, with ruffles, folds and maybe pleats. Nothing is tight. Everything will flow and move as she walks.

The feminine style personality loves shoes. She loves ballet slippers, sandals and court shoes and has shoes in a lot of different colours and styles. She loves to wear lace and silk lingerie and matching sets of underwear. Her jewellery is soft, small, delicate pieces. She won't wear anything that's big, chunky and makes a statement. She does like to add a bit of sparkle and loves small pearls. Her watch will be quite small, and perhaps a bracelet style. The feminine style personality loves to wear glasses with metal, perhaps with a floral design. She might prefer the rimless glasses that are very subtle in design. She likes to wear light-coloured handbags, such as cream or pink. Quite often, her handbag will have soft gathering with a little bit of gold or silver. She might have some bows or ruffles on her handbags or clutch purses.

Chapter 7 - Being You

Elegant

The elegant style personality is quite often combined with the relaxed Style. She likes to wear quality clothing without a lot of fuss. Where the classic style personality likes to wear a jacket that's quite structured, the elegant style personality prefers a more draped, flowing style. They like to look feminine and also relaxed. Even though her styling does take time, it looks effortless.

The elegant style personality always has neat hair, which could have soft curls or is just smooth. Her makeup is always going to be subtle and well applied. She always looks well-groomed with fabrics like cashmere and silk. She wears dresses and trousers in neutral colours, like caramels and creams, which she may pair with the medium-coloured neutrals or darker colours. She also likes to wear solid colours. If she does wear prints, they're stylized or geometric prints. The elegant style personality could best be described as having a streamlined look. It's also soft and drapey. Everything will flow – she loves that flowing movement as she walks. She likes to go to the high-end boutiques and enjoys a little bit of subtle bling, maybe in the form of buckles and belts. The elegant style personality likes a modern look to her jewellery. The frame shape of her glasses and sunglasses is clean and striking. Like the classic style personality, she uses a leather handbag and her pen and accessories will be good quality.

Chapter 7 - Being You

Action Steps

Have a look in your wardrobe and see if there is a particular pattern in the garments you have:

— Do you have mainly neutral colours and classic styles?

— Do you have structured jackets and dresses? Skirts or pants with lots of zips? Dramatic geometric patterns?

— Do you have garments with creative mixtures of stripes and florals, complementary (opposite colours) and unusual details?

— Do you have a lot of relaxed and comfortable tracksuits, casual jeans, sweat tops, T-shirts?

— Do you have lots of black garments, with zips and studs and rebellious style graphic art designs?

— Do you have a lot of feminine florals and frills with flowing tops and jackets?

— Do you have elegant flowing styles of jackets, dresses and pants?

Resources

Discover how your psychological type (Myers Briggs) and personality influence your style:
https://16styletypes.com
Clinical psychologist Dr. Jennifer Baumgartner: "You Are What You Wear: What Your Clothes Reveal About You"

8. Bold and Beautiful

Smiling Eyes

"Smile with your eyes". I've heard photographers use this expression so many times. How you're feeling does show through your eyes. You can fake a smile, but if you're not happy, glowing and full of vitality, it will show through in your eyes. Look at the science of Iridology and how much an Iridologist can tell from looking at your eyes.

Your eyes show your health. They show your emotions. They're usually the main focal point when you're having a one-on-one conversation with someone. It's a great compliment for someone to notice the colour of your eyes. This is why image consultants and personal stylists tell clients what colours are going to be their "eye-enhancing colours". These are the colours that really make your eyes pop. It's something I notice a lot now as a personal stylist. If I am sitting at a table full of people and talking to them, I always notice their eyes.

Whether you're in business or not, the goal is to have the person you're talking with drawn to your eyes. You can tell a lot about someone by their eyes. There are so many different eye shapes and colours. There is also the movement: how many times you blink, how you focus or whether you have your eyes slightly closed when talking to someone. Have you noticed how a person's eyes sparkle when they are excited or happy?

Just like our fingerprints, the iris of our eyes varies from person to person. The exciting part is, the visual shape of your eyes can actually be enhanced, changed or accentuated using eye makeup.

How Much Makeup?

If you don't like wearing a lot of makeup, I would recommend finding out what type of light foundations or tinted moisturisers you are comfortable wearing and stick with these. There are products such as CC or BB creams, which are tinted moisturisers you can use if you don't like wearing a lot of makeup. Quite often, just one of those creams as a foundation, some mascara and some lipstick or lip gloss is enough, depending on your lifestyle and style personality. Mineral powders are also easy to apply and can be layered.

If you love wearing makeup, go for it! Have fun and experiment. There is no reason you shouldn't enjoy being creative and try out different brands and styles of makeup at any age. You can get the look you want with some clever makeup tips.

Our facial features vary so much from person to person. There are tips and tricks to highlight and minimise different areas. As we get older 'less is more' when it comes to makeup. It pays to work out what colours suit you and restrain from overdoing it, as subtle and light will be more flattering on older skin.

Chapter 8 - Bold And Beautiful

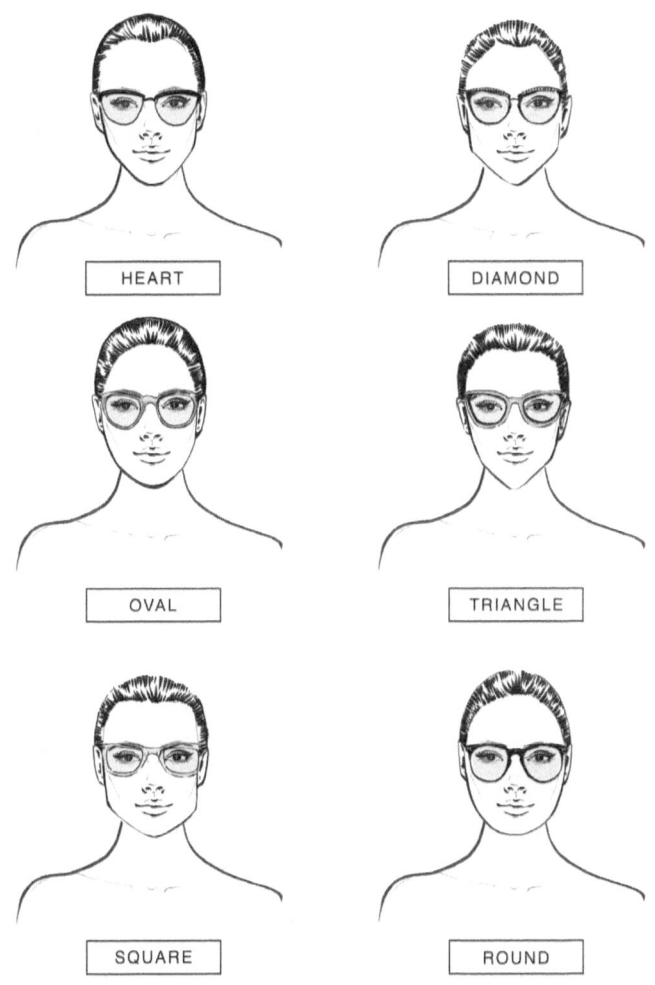

Sunnies And Spectacles

As we age, we may need to wear glasses for reading. We also need to wear sunglasses, because our eyes can actually get sunburned, the same way the rest of our body can. Most women find it difficult to choose glasses to suit their face shape. Glasses can look so attractive if chosen carefully. They can even be a stand out accessory if you are someone who likes to make a statement.

20/20 Vision

One year, I went and had my eyes tested at the optometrist. He said I had 20/20 vision. This doesn't mean perfect vision, although it sounded like that to me. It just means you have average vision for someone your age. The following year, I went and had my eyes tested and found I needed glasses, so it can happen suddenly. It's really important to choose glasses that flatter your face shape.

My focus for this chapter is the shape of your glasses and how to choose a pair to flatter your face shape. I will also give you tips about makeup, hairstyles and necklines for each face shape.

Questions Clients Ask

Some clients say to me, "I have an asymmetrical face shape. One side of my face is slightly different to the other side of the face". There are some tips and tricks you can use for this, which include wearing clothing that is slightly asymmetrical as well. This means opting for asymmetrical hemlines, patterns which aren't structured, or patterns which are quite random.

Some clients ask me how they can slim their face down. There are ways you can do this using shading. Use a slightly darker foundation on the sides of your face and shading under your chin, as well as down the sides of your forehead. You can use a darker shade of foundation, or a shading cream, like a bronzer.

Just as clothing colours can be ascending (visually coming forward) if they are light and receding (visually going backwards) if they are dark, the same works for shading and highlighting with makeup. This is why makeup artists can do so much with contouring. You can highlight cheekbones by adding a lighter colour to make them protrude more visually and shading underneath the cheekbone with a darker colour to create more of a hollow.

Heart

Let's start with the heart face shape. This is sometimes referred to as the 'Inverted Triangle'. Your face will be wider at the temple and go down to a slightly narrower chin. You might have a widow's peak, and if you think of an actual heart shape, you will see that shape when you pull your hair back.

You want to create balance and keep some fullness and softness at the jawline. That's where the bulk of your hair should be. Layers are going to be good for your face shape. Chin-length bobs, where it's fuller down the bottom, are going to suit you. Anything cropped at the side, and a fringe or fullness on the top of your head, is going to accentuate the heart shape of your face. A side-swept fringe may suit you.

Go for a V or sweetheart neckline in your clothing. It's best to avoid crew necks. With makeup, you can add a bit of blush to your temples. Make sure your eyebrows are gently curved and keep away from any harsh angles. With jewellery, you can wear earrings that are wider at the base, such as fan-shaped earrings, or something that's rounded, but wide at the base.

Glasses with delicate round or square frames with low sides are going to suit heart-shaped faces.

Diamond

Your cheekbones are the widest part of your face and you have a narrow forehead and chin area. You suit soft, wavy hair styles and a fringe is also going to look good. Avoid any styles that are cut close to the face and angular. Choose wide or narrow V necks, sweetheart and cowl necklines. Softly angle your eyebrows. Some highlighting of your brow bone with makeup and around the sides of the jawline will even out your face shape. You can shade the tip of your chin with a darker shade or no-shine bronzer. Earrings that are wider at the base will be flattering.

Glasses frames which are deeper than they are wide will suit you.

Triangular

Your jawline will be wider than your forehead, which will be quite narrow. Choose a hairstyle with fullness and softness at the top, as it will balance out your face shape. Side or off-centre parts will suit you best. Avoid hairstyles that finish near the jawline. Necklines in garments with round shapes will suit you. You can apply some no-shine bronzer or a darker shade of foundation to the jawline. Make sure your eyebrows are well defined, especially in the arch. Drop and long dangly earrings will look great on you.

Glasses that have bold detail and wide shapes will suit you.

Oval and Oblong

With the oval face shape or an oblong face shape (which is slightly longer), you're going to look great with a fringe or side parts and layers around your ears or waves around your face – anything to soften your face and add some bulk to the sides. An oval is considered the perfect face shape, so any hair style is going to suit you. If you have an oblong shape, where you've got length to your face, it's best to avoid the long, straight hairdo, as this will only drag your face down. You need body in your hair if it's going to be long.

Depending on the rest of your body shape, you can use higher necklines. No matter what face shape you have, it's always best to match the neckline to the shape of your jaw. Wide soft V necklines are going to look really good on you. Use your blusher to dust from your cheekbones up to your temples. You can also dust along your jawline with some contouring powder, like a non-shiny bronzer, or a darker shade of foundation. This can shorten your jawline.

If you flatten your eyebrows out, your face is going to appear a little bit wider. For jewellery, choose earrings that are wider rather than longer, to help balance your face. You can wear your earrings a little bit shorter as well.

Chapter 8 - Bold And Beautiful

Just about any frames will suit the oval face shape. You can try angular or modern aviator frames. Make sure to take note of the size of your face and the size of the glasses. If you have a small face, keep glasses within the range of the sides of your face.

Square

The square face shape has strong angular lines. You have a strong jaw and it will be quite obvious your face shape is square.

If you've got straight hair, try add some softness and body around your face. You could do this by getting some layers. A side part really suits a square face shape, because it's going to add an asymmetrical look, and you can either add some height or length to your style. Strong, sharp angular lines in a haircut will accentuate a square face shape. Try to keep your hairstyles soft and layered. It's a good idea to have your hair finishing away from your jaw line. Wherever your hair finishes creates a horizontal line, which draws the attention to your square jawline. If you've got a really dramatic personality, you may want to accentuate your face shape, so remember all these tips are personal choice.

With a square face shape, square necklines are going to look good, as will boat necklines and wide, soft square necklines, which have slight curves at the corners.

If you contour your temples and your cheeks with some blush or bronzer, this will soften the outside of your jawline. Add a little bit of length to your eyebrows and soften them to create some balance to your square face. You can create some arches in your brows that are directly over your jawline. Long, narrow earrings will look great, because they'll balance your face shape.

Square-framed glasses with rounded corners to soften will suit your face. The glasses should sit high on the face to soften the jawline.

Round

Your face is equally wide as it is long and you'll have that beautiful soft fullness to your cheekbones. If you want to contour your face to make it look more oval, narrower and longer, then add some darker foundation to the sides of your cheeks. Don't bring your shading further up than the outside of your eyes. The idea is to create a shadow and more protruding cheekbones. A good tip is to find your cheekbone, hold your index finger downwards along the cheekbone and apply the shadow or bronzer under this. You can add a slight amount of blusher along the top of this line.

A classic bob hairstyle is going to make your face look even rounder. You can wear a centre part if you've got long hair, as long as your hair falls below your chin. If you can, wear your hair pulled back, or off to the side. With the necklines, match the curve of your jaw to the curve of your neckline. Look for round scoop or cowl necklines.

To make your face appear thinner and longer, create some height on your brows by arching your brow line further out to the side. Jewellery can be longer, drop earrings to balance out your rounder face.

Longer frames with high sides and detail near the temples will suit your face and slim the jawline.

A Word About Eyebrows

They really do frame the face and it's important to make sure they are well groomed and filled in. You can get your eyebrows tattooed, which can look quite natural. Make sure you check out the cosmetic tattoo artist and their pre-work procedure. It's important they take the time to ensure you are happy with the shape and the colour. Check their before and after photographs and ask around for testimonials. It's all personal preference and a lot of people, like myself, have had their eyebrows filled in with eyebrow tattooing. I had this done because

Chapter 8 - Bold And Beautiful

I over plucked them when I was younger. As you get older, if your eyesight is going, it's best to have this professionally done. If you're colouring your eyebrows, your brows should be similar to the colour of your hair. Take notice of your complexion colour, because you want them to look natural. Just do it in layers, start off lightly and increase the darkness of your eyebrow colour until you get the right shade.

Skincare

Diet plays an important part in the health of your skin and eyes. If you want nice, fresh, glowing skin and eyes, no matter what age you are, then look after your diet. Drinking lots of water helps with hydration, and if you have red skin and broken capillaries, avoid too many hot spicy foods and too much alcohol.

My mum still has beautiful skin at the age she is. She instilled in me to never use harsh soap on my face. I remember when I was young she showed me a cake of soap on a wooden window sill, lifted it up and said, "Look at what this soap does to the paint on the window sill. It takes it off". Then she told me about using soap on your face. I know we don't have paint on our face, but it demonstrates how harsh ordinary soap can be on the skin.

Use something that's intended for cleansing the skin on your face. It doesn't always need to be the most expensive product, but you will soon tell if you're wearing or using something that doesn't agree with your skin. If you're using a product with a lot of active ingredients, without a whole lot of cheap fillers, you may find a slight tingling or redness to your skin. This can mean the product is quite active and should calm down in a few days.

A simple way to tell whether you've got dry, oily or combination skin, is by the look of it. If you have that sheen or shine on your skin halfway through the day, you probably have normal to oily skin. Sometimes we have a slightly oily T-zone, which is the forehead, nose and chin.

If you wash your face or get out of the shower in the morning and feel your skin tightening up and feel that you need to put moisturiser on straightaway, this means you have very dry skin. As we get older, our skin does tend to be dry rather than oily. Night creams are important, as our skin cells renew faster when we are asleep and it ensures your skin is fed while this happens.

It's just as important as ever at this age to cleanse, tone and moisturise with good quality products. Eye creams are lighter than normal moisturisers and it's important to treat the delicate eye area differently to the rest of the face. I'm not a believer in the wrinkle remover gels, as they are only a temporary fix and can stretch the skin. They are cosmetic rather than skincare.

When writing this book, I asked my clients for questions they wanted addressed. One of the concerns they had was wrinkles and bags around the eyes. I really do believe that using a good eye cream works. It's important you don't put the cream too close to the eye – apply it around the orbital bone and the cream will work its way to where it's needed. We have less oil around the eyes and lips. If you have any eye cream left over after applying, put it around your lips. With regard to puffiness under the eyes, I have found that cucumber slices and cold camomile tea bags work. This is an at-home trick, and something anyone can use. Apart from regular skincare routines, it's important to exfoliate a couple of times a week, depending on your skin type.

Find a good beauty therapist you enjoy going to and strike up a relationship, so you can trust her to look after your skin. She will also help to point out anything you've got coming up on your skin, such as any sunspots she thinks you should go and see your doctor or dermatologist about to get a sun check done. It really is important to look after your skin, and of course, to always wear sunscreen if you're going to be outside, especially for prolonged periods of time during the day.

Sunscreen

While on the subject of sunscreen, you should be wearing at least SPF 15+ every day. If you are outdoors a lot, then SPF 30+ should be applied, which means it would take you 30 more times to burn than if you wore no sunscreen. Make sure your day cream has a sunscreen built in. Whatever you put on the top layer is what counts towards SPF, as it isn't cumulative. For example, if you are wearing a day cream with SPF 20+ and foundation with SPF 15+, you will only have SPF 15+ protection, not SPF 30+ sun protection factor. It needs to be re-applied every 30 minutes if you are in in the sun.

The three most ageing factors for the skin – sun, smoking and stress.

Action Steps

1. See if you can work out what face shape you have from the descriptions above. If you haven't already done this, you may be surprised at the difference it makes to use some of the tips mentioned.

2. Go through your bathroom cupboards and throw out any skincare and makeup that's out of date, as old makeup and skincare can be harmful to your skin if it contains bacteria.

3. Take some time out to give yourself a facial or make an appointment to have one. You are worth it!

4. Have professional makeup done to refresh your ideas and maybe get some completely new tips and tricks. Notice what you like about the results and try replicating that at home.

9.
Black is not a colour

There are so many debates around this statement. Technically, black isn't a colour – nor is it a shade. We commonly refer to it as a colour as it's easier. Black is the absence of light. It's the absorption of all colour. I've chosen black to start this conversation about colour, because so many of my clients, for a variety of reasons, say they tend to wear nothing but black.

Techy Terms Of Colour

Although technically black is the absence of light and the absorption of all colours, I refer to black as a colour in this chapter. I'm going to define some of the technical terms:

- A hue is the pure form of what is normally called a colour.
- A tint is a colour with white added to it.
- Shade is a colour with black added to it.
- Tone is mixing grey to a colour.
- The value of a colour is whether it is light or dark.

Advancing And Receding

Many people do hide behind black as it's receding. You see lighter colours first, as these are advancing. A lot of people wear black to look slimmer. If you're not careful how you wear black, it can actually make you look heavier. It can be slimming if there isn't too much material and it isn't a voluminous garment.

Dark colours do actually minimise areas of your body you would like to take the attention away from. So, if you are bigger down the bottom half of your body, it's good to wear darker coloured trousers, pants, or skirts. If you feel you'd like to minimise the top part of your body, then this is where you wear the dark colours.

Cool Shades

If you have warm colouring, you usually don't look as good in black as those with cool undertones. It can drain the colour from your face and highlight imperfections or facial redness. I personally love black and I know a lot of other women do, too. So, how do you wear black if you don't suit it?

- Wear it away from your face.
- Wear lacy or sheer fabric on the top that shows skin through. This softens the black.
- Wear a scarf or necklace in one of your colours to distract from the black.

Neutrals

A lot of women feel more professional when they're wearing black. Other neutral colours also achieve this look, such as navy blue, charcoal, aubergine and dark chocolate brown. I think navy is a great replacement for black. As I have changed my hair from a very dark colour to a very

Chapter 9 - Black Is Not A Colour

light colour, I've had to redo my whole colour palette. I now tend to go for navy or dark blues rather than black.

As well as looking at the hue, tint, shade, or tone, other factors come into play, such as whether colours are bright, clear, soft and muted, dark or light. If colours have a toasty look, this means they've got some brown added. Pastel colours have a tint, as they have some white added. Adding grey to a colour gives it a smokiness.

> *"The best colour in the whole world is the one that looks good on you."*
>
> **– Coco Chanel**

Let's go through the psychology of colour. Most of you are probably aware of the impact that colour has on us in our everyday life. When you think about it, we use a word to describe colour about 10 to 15 times a day, or more. It would be interesting to count up how many times in our day we mention a colour. We use it to describe someone, something, or a point of interest. For example, if we need someone to go and talk to a specific person, we may say, "that woman over there in the red dress", or point out that "blue building over there".

Black

Black can look dignified. It has been traditional to wear black to a funeral, as it looks sombre and is seen as a sign of respect (some cultures have different colours for this). Black looks cosmopolitan – you notice it in a lot of cities like Melbourne and New York. When I went back to New Zealand, I noticed so many people in Wellington wear black. Of course there is the culture and loyalty to the All Black Rugby Team! Also, who doesn't love the little black dress!

One negative of black is that it can be too solemn. It's quite formal and can be seen as standoffish and cold looking. So, if you want to appear approachable, it's probably best not to wear black. Traditionally, not many people wore black to weddings, although this does seem to be changing in more recent times.

White

White stands for purity. It's a clean looking colour – a lot of hospitals and clinics use white in their décor and uniforms. It makes other colours stand out, so it's a good contrast. It can make you look browner if you are tanned in Summer. White can be very modern looking.

On the negative side, white can be quite clinical looking and sometimes bland. If you're someone who doesn't have a lot of time for washing and taking care of your clothing, think twice before wearing white. White does show a lot of marks. Even slightly leaning up against a dusty car or brushing against objects with dirt on them can mark white garments.

Red

Red is a power colour. It can be very dramatic and have a lot of impact. There was one woman I knew who always used to wear red if she was going into an important meeting and wanted to create an impact when she walked into the room. She would normally wear black suits and swap that out for red on important meeting days. Red is quite an energetic colour, so it's popular in gymnasiums or where people are doing a lot of weight lifting, or strength training. You may see more pastel or soft colours at a Yoga or Pilates class. Red can demonstrate authority.

The negatives of red are that it can look as though you're being too bold and too out there. Not all reds are flattering, so it's important to know whether you suit the warm reds or the cool reds. A lot of restaurants use red in their colour scheme, because red is said to increase the appetite.

Chapter 9 - Black Is Not A Colour

Blue

You will find blue in lot of logos for banks, as it's a colour that promotes trust. The police have blue in their colour scheme and it can promote a sense of reliability and dependability. A negative of blue is that it can be a bit boring. I'm personally a fan of blue, because I feel there are so many different, complementary shades that make you look good, and so many different types of warm or cool blues.

Brown

Brown is a colour that has a lot of different shades. You can have warm browns and cool browns, but it's usually a warm colour. Not many cool-toned people can wear brown successfully. Brown is a colour that looks earthy. It can be a welcoming, nice and natural colour. However, it can also look a bit drab or boring. The best way to wear brown is with other colours, such as whites or creams. If you have warm colouring, brown looks fantastic with different shades of beige or tan. Brown is not a colour that's as popular as some of the other colours.

Pink

Normally classed as delicate or feminine, pink is often used to create a softer appearance. The negatives of pink are that can be a bit insipid and insignificant unless it's super bright. It can be quite a girly colour, but a lot of men are starting to wear pink now too and some really suit it. There are lots of different shades of pink – you have hot pink, pastel pinks, coral pinks, and more.

Yellow

As a bright, happy, friendly colour, yellow reminds us of sunshine and fun times. A lot of my clients have said they avoid yellow. Some people can look stunning in yellow, but whether you suit it or not depends on if it's a cool yellow or a warm yellow. The negatives are that it isn't a colour to wear if you want to be make a serious impression. It can also be a hard colour to wear unless it's in your colour palette.

Green

Another colour with many variations. You instantly think of nature when you see it, so it can promote a sense of reliability and friendliness. If you see someone wearing green, it's normally because they like to look natural. It can be quite a calming colour to wear. Green can be a beautiful, cool colour in some of the rich jewel variations, like jade green. Yellow greens are for the warmer skin tones. These can look so bright and fresh. Dark green is usually associated with money. The downside is that people sometimes associate this with negative emotions, such as jealousy or even illness.

Orange

One positive of orange is that it's dynamic. Creative people often like to wear orange with purple. It's highly visible, which is why a lot of workers around machinery wear orange in uniforms or vests.

Orange can also signify someone who's flighty or volatile. It can be quite a playful, fun colour and make you look impulsive. Burnt orange is a colour that cool-toned people shouldn't be wearing. It's beautiful on warm-toned people.

Purple

A lot of creative people love to wear purple. It shows you're unique and can also be a serene colour. Purple has traditionally been associated with royalty. It evokes feelings of mystery and magic. I find a lot of

Chapter 9 - Black Is Not A Colour

alternative therapies use purple in their logos. Beautiful mauves are purple with the tint of white added. Purples can go well with so many other colours. Purple projects confidence and shows you as being an individual. The negatives are that purple is sometimes associated with frustration and dark purple can evoke sadness or gloominess.

Grey

Ah yes, there probably are Fifty Shades of Grey! Warm greys, cool greys, blue greys, light greys, dark greys, brown greys... The list goes on. As part of a workshop group delivering confidence and style classes for women, we wanted a theme colour and clothing colour for the presenters to wear. Grey is a wonderful neutral and goes well with other colours. I suggested grey dresses with aqua and turquoise accessories. This way, all presenters suited their outfits, no matter whether they were warm or cool. They chose the particular grey which suited them. Grey gives the indication that someone's calm and reliable. The negative about grey is it can look a bit insipid, detached, cool or cold, and it can look very businesslike. Personally, as I associate grey with business and offices, it's not a colour I like to use a lot of in furniture at home. I like it when it's combined with other colours.

When we're thinking about colours and the effect they have on us and others, we need to keep in mind how bright the colours are, their clarity and whether they're muted or not. Think about how you feel when wearing different colours.

Bright, clear colours usually have high contrast. They suit women with high contrast in their skin-tone and features. If you think of someone like Elizabeth Taylor, she had that bright, clear colour contrast. The pale skin, very vivid eyes, very dark hair. If we think of light colours, these have low contrast with soft, muted complexions and hair. Someone with blonde or lighter coloured hair is going to be classed as a light. If their eye colour is light and their skin tone is light, then they are low contrast. If someone has dark skin, dark eyes and dark hair, they would also be classed as low contrast.

Muted colouring is where there is not such a distinct change between one colour and the other. Even if you're wearing two or more colours together, they could quite easily blend into each other and don't have such a strong distinct contrast.

Someone who has a cool colouring is easy to distinguish. Think of water and the sky. People with definite cool colourings don't suit any shade of orange. The warm-coloured undertones make you think of the sun, Summer, Autumn and autumn leaves, beaches, sand and florals. Anybody who looks like they've got a warmth about them. Think of fire. Warm-toned people suit oranges, browns, tans, and anything that's got warmth. They usually will have brown, red or golden blonde hair. Sometimes they might have what's called strawberry blonde hair.

When it comes to hair colour, it's really important to ensure your hair colour complements your skin tone. When we reach this magical age, it's hard to blend greys in if you've got dark hair. If you've got blonde hair, it's a lot easier to blend the greys and to get away with a few more weeks before having your colour redone. Some people like to just go grey naturally and others are lucky enough to just have that beautiful white, silver colour. I went lighter as I started to go very grey. Having dark hair and going to the hairdresser more often became a real bind. I went lighter and lighter over a period of months. I did it very gradually with the help of a great hairdresser.

It's important to keep an eye on brassiness if you're naturally dark and go blonde or lighter. As you are advancing in years, it's important to take care of that brassiness if you are in the cool colouring group. If you have warm skin tone, it's not as important, because the brassiness quite often suits. Hence why cool undertones suit silver jewellery and warm undertones suit gold jewellery – the same applies to hair. So, a warm blonde would be someone who has honey, strawberry, auburn, golden brown hair and they will suit that type of hair.

Chapter 9 - Black Is Not A Colour

Cool skin-toned people with dark hair who start to go grey are going to look their best if they go to the ash tones if going a lot lighter. If they keep their dark hair, and especially if they have that really, really dark black hair, it's best to soften that colour by going a bit lighter – maybe a dark chocolate brown. As we age, our skin gets lighter as well and black as a contrast to the pale skin can be very harsh. Contrast levels are important when it comes to colouring your hair.

An interesting exercise is to take a look at the newsreaders on TV and notice if they're wearing the wrong colour for them. For example, someone with very blonde hair who wears black can just look like a head floating on shoulders. What you wear should look harmonious with all of you. Look at the whole picture.

You will notice the difference colour can make after reading this chapter. You will notice if everything looks harmonious and blended, or whether the clothing stands out more than the person. The idea is for the eyes to be drawn up to the face of the other person. That's where you want people to focus when you're talking to them. You don't want them to see your red dress before they see you. But if red is one of your great signature colours, then you're going to look harmonious.

To keep it nice and simple, the starting point is to work out if you have light or dark colouring, and then whether you have a warm or cool undertone. Then work out whether there is a lot of difference between your skin, hair and eye colours. After that, go into what colours suit you.

Action Steps

Depth of Colour - work out whether your colouring is light or dark (light or dark hair and overall appearance).

Undertone – work out whether your skin tone is warm or cool. If you are warm, you will suit the gold colours, and if you are cool, you will suit silver. Go into your wardrobe and find an item of clothing which is cream and another one that is white. Hold each up against your face and take a really good look in the light and work out whether your skin looks clearer and fresher if you have the cream underneath your chin or the white. You can take a piece of gold and silver jewellery or material and do exactly the same thing. People who have a neutral undertone will be able to wear gold and silver successfully

Contrast – work out whether your appearance is clear or muted. You do this by looking at your features (without makeup on). Are your eyes and your lips brighter and more of a contrast to the skin on your face? If everything blends, then look at your face from a distance and if your eyes and lips aren't as easily distinguishable from your skin colour, it means you have a softer or more muted colouring. If you have very, very distinct features, such as dark eyes and dark lips with white skin, then you could possibly be a high contrast person. You can have high contrast whether you have light or dark hair, it all depends on the difference between your hair, eyes and skin colour.

Chapter 9 - Black Is Not A Colour

Resources

Download a Warm or Cool Clothing and Accessory Tip Sheet from the link below:
www.bstyledforlife.com.au/resources
Password is Style50

10. Benefits of Choice

Five Minute Find

My dad used to say, "A place for everything, and everything in its place". This rings true with me today with the work I do. The idea of a wardrobe audit is that you should be able to reach in and select out what you want to wear within about five minutes.

What you've chosen to wear will look fabulous on you, because everything in your wardrobe should suit your style and your body shape and should be the right colour for you.

Here are the benefits:

- Save time and stress when choosing your outfits.
- Rediscover clothing that you didn't know you had.
- Save money not needing to buy entire new outfits.
- Sell or donate the unneeded clothes to someone who might need them.

The Cost In More Than $$

Most women spend 90 minutes a week deciding what to wear, and only actually wear 20% of their wardrobe. The other 80% of their wardrobe is taking up 'rent free space'. The reason I say rent free space, is it actually takes up a lot of time and energy to go through clothes you don't wear and probably don't intend to wear. This comes at a cost to your time and energy.

A Sad Fact

You may miss out on some of the good things in life. You may even avoid going out. I had one client who used to hesitate before going on dinner dates with her husband because she just didn't know what to wear. She used to refuse invitations to social events for the same reason. She didn't know where to start. There are two issues that most people have:

(1) Some feel they don't have any clothes to suit them. They feel they don't have enough clothes.

(2) Some people have too many clothes and don't know even where to start selecting an outfit.

It's A Matter Of Choice

These seem to be two different types of problems, but actually it all comes down to the same thing. It's a matter of choice. Personally, I like it when I go away on holiday, taking a suitcase of some of my favourite clothes, and only having a few clothes to choose from.

This is a situation I enjoy on a temporary basis. If this was how I had to live and dress in my normal day-to-day life, I wouldn't like it. I usually like to be able to go into my wardrobe and dress according to whatever mood I'm in at the time.

Chapter 10 - Benefits Of Choice

Style Challenge

I've enjoyed taking part in a style challenge, where I give myself a few minutes to go into the wardrobe and find what I need to wear for that particular challenge. It could be something like, wear stripes with spots. I would go into my wardrobe, find something with stripes, something with spots and wear that for the day. Another challenge was to choose the pair of shoes first and then get dressed from the shoes upwards. The idea was to make your outfit look complete according to what shoes you were wearing. I appreciated the opportunity to be part of this challenge and had fun with it.

Overwhelm

Some people may be overwhelmed with too much choice in their wardrobe. There have been studies and experiments carried out to do with choice. One group of participants were given a choice of 30 types of chocolate. Another group could choose from six types of chocolate.

While subjects initially reported liking the choice of 30 chocolates, they actually ended up being more dissatisfied and regretful of their choice. They would have preferred to have a choice of only six. People wonder if they have made the right choice when they have too much to choose from. We like to have some choice, but not too much.

This can come into play when you're choosing clothes from your wardrobe. If you're going to a special event, are you happy with the outfit you've chosen or do you get to the event and wish you had chosen something else?

Think of going to a restaurant with one of those exhaustively large menus. It can be off-putting. Then the other extreme is a restaurant where the menu is too limited. This leaves us wanting more choice. How about that 'food envy' when you see what someone else has ordered – have you experienced this? You may have heard of FOMO

(Fear Of Missing Out). Did you know about FOBO (Fear Of a Better Offer)? This can come into play when you have a lot of clothes and try to make a decision about what to wear to an event.

Complexity Of Choice

The multimillion dollar company Shoes of Prey collapsed in March 2019 for a few reasons – one of them being that they were trying to keep the customers happy with too much choice. They gave customers the unique ability to design their own shoes in virtually every aspect, such as colour, style, heel, toe and decorations. It was reported that customers found the 'complexity of choice' overwhelming as the range got larger and larger.

Streamlining your wardrobe with just the right amount of choice for you and your personality is important.

Have Fun Getting Dressed

When you know what suits you, what clothes you have in your wardrobe, and how to put those clothes together, then you will always be happy with how you look when you walk out that door. The idea is to have fun when you're getting dressed, to really enjoy the challenge of looking the best you possibly can. You may have too many clothes in your wardrobe like I did when my daughters left home. I had two spare double wardrobes that I could quite easily fill up and there was no need for me to downsize.

Look At The Reasons For Hanging On

If you find that you just can't possibly throw anything away, have a look at the reasons you're hanging onto these garments. I've had clients tell me they can't throw something away in case they wear it again. I

Chapter 10 - Benefits Of Choice

suggest they put the garments or accessories aside in a bag or a box for 12 months. If they haven't used them within those 12 months, then completely get rid of them.

I've also had clients say they're emotionally attached to items. They've been given something as a gift from someone, or they've been given an item of clothing where the person it is from is emotionally attached to them. I suggest working out where the attachment comes from and possibly giving it to another family member or friend who would love to have it, or you can take a photo of that garment to keep the memory of it.

Think about the beginning of this chapter. Do you want to have a lot of options, or do you want to have a minimalist wardrobe? Do you want to streamline your wardrobe so you can quickly be ready for any occasion?

Here are some of these reasons to declutter your wardrobe:

- To actually see all your clothes so you know what you have.
- To find the gaps in your wardrobe, so when you go shopping for clothes, they're items you really do need, not just impulse buying.
- You may want to eliminate the clutter and get rid of some double-ups, for example, 10 pairs of black pants.

You can achieve all these things by following a very simple process.

Choosing What Goes And What Stays

So how do you go about Spring cleaning or decluttering your wardrobe? The exercise of thinking about, analysing and dividing the clothes and accessories into three piles is my secret to decluttering a wardrobe.

Start with your hanging items, and keep your situation in mind, including your current lifestyle and your goals for your wardrobe.

The Secret To A Simple Wardrobe Declutter

Your goal is to declutter and put the clothes you are keeping in places where it's easier to find them. Take each item out of the wardrobe and ask yourself the following questions:

— Is it the right shape?
— Is it the right colour?
— Does it reflect my personality?
— Is the garment suitable for my current lifestyle?

If you answer yes to all these questions, hang that garment back up.

If you answer no to any of them:

— Could it be made to fit by altering it, or does it need repair or mending?

If yes, put this item into a pile for mending or altering.

If you answer no to all of the above:

— Is it in good condition? If it is, put it aside for donating or selling.
— If it's not in good condition, put it into a bag for disposing of.

All the 'yes' items will be back in the wardrobe neatly, and the 'no' items will be in one of three piles or bags.

Repeat all these steps until you've gone through your whole wardrobe, including your drawers, baskets and shelves, and each pair of shoes and all your accessories.

In my online program and 'Wardrobe Organising Workbook', which you can download from my website, I name these three piles/bags/baskets Dump, Donate and Darn.

Chapter 10 - Benefits Of Choice

1. Dump Basket: for getting rid of clothes.
2. Donate Basket: for giving away clothes.
3. Darn Basket: for mending or altering clothes.*

It seems simple, but it does make a difference. The secret is to ask yourself as you go through each question: "Why don't I wear this?", and not, "What will I do with this now?". You need to make the process fast so you don't get frozen by procrastination, throw your hands up in the air and think, "Oh, it's just all too hard"…and shove everything back into the wardrobe!

Think Of The Goal You Started With

Don't give up. Each time you feel frustrated or overwhelmed, think of the goal you first started with. Also think of this as a discovery experience, because you might be surprised at what you discover you actually have and haven't worn for ages. You could discover a whole new outfit. You can learn a lot about yourself and your own style by going through this process. Think about how each garment makes you feel. Think about whether it still fits with your lifestyle. This can help working out of it's your style or not, and also with categorising it.

Do They Make The Grade?

If this garment makes the grade for you and stays in your wardrobe, that's great. Now everything in your wardrobe, drawers and baskets, you love and feel good in, and it suits you, your shape, colouring and lifestyle. If you have a few problems deciding whether to keep something or not, ask yourself, "If I saw this in the shop, would I buy it again?"

Each item in your wardrobe serves a purpose. You know that you're definitely going to wear it. This is your personal wardrobe. Once you've

---

* Interesting that one of my younger clients hadn't heard the word 'darn' used before.

been through all the garments and items, think about what you now have available to wear.

Easy Access

Whether your wardrobe is small or large, you need to ask yourself, "How easy is it to get to the clothes I want to get to in a hurry?". For example, if you get up early in the morning and go walking or to the gym, these clothes need to be easily accessible. Our eyes instinctively look from left to right. What you wear regularly should be on the left side of your wardrobe. What is worn only occasionally should be on the right.

Think about this, do you have Winter clothes mixed in with Summer clothes? Or do you have space to store out-of-season clothes somewhere else? Just stop for a minute and look at the lifestyle you have now, and this will help you recognise what clothes are needed in your wardrobe and what clothes aren't. If there are any gaps, you can make note of these for you next shopping trip.

Identify what you use different types of clothing for. You might want to make a note of smart casual, social, dinners, barbecues, lunch with friends, coffee meetings, and so on, depending on your lifestyle. You'll see what needs to be easily accessible depending on how often those items are used.

Categorise those items in different areas of your wardrobe.

Different activity areas need to be accessible, depending on how quickly you need to get to them.

Then further categorise by grouping different items together:

- Skirts
- Pants

Chapter 10 - Benefits Of Choice

- Tops
- Shirts and jackets

I further categorise again with knit tops, T-shirts and camisoles.

Hang each category up in blocks of colours. If you don't have space for a belt hanger, a drawer can be used with a rubber band placed around each belt to keep them tidy.

Jewellery hanging bags are great and make your fashion jewellery really easy to see. You can go to a storage shop like Howards Storage World, which has some great ideas. There are lots of items like this available online as well. I have fashion jewellery colour-coded into each pocket of a jewellery hanging bag.

Here are some other suggestions:

- Jewellery tidy racks that can be bought from hardware stores or online.
- Over-the-door hooks are great for scarves.
- Accessory hangers from Spotlight or online.
- Shoe bags, which can be pockets on hangers or clear storage boxes.
- Shoe racks and boot hangers.
- Ice-cube trays to keep earrings together.
- Coffee mug trees for necklaces.
- Plate stacking rack to organise clutch purses.

I take photos of some of my shoes and put a photo on the outside of the shoe box to store them in. It keeps the shoes nice and clean. You wouldn't believe how much time this saves. It also cuts out the expense of buying those clear plastic shoe boxes, hangers, bags or racks. It depends how many shoes you have – and how much shelf space.

When I first started organising my wardrobe, I gradually replaced all my odd hangers with black hangers with hooks for clothes, which have shoulder straps and hanging tapes. I use wooden hangers for my husband's trousers, because they're nice and sturdy, and trousers don't get the vertical creases on them as they hang straight from the wooden hanger.

The ultra-slim, velvet hangers are really good if you're short on space, and they grip well so that the straps on garments don't slip off. I have baskets for exercise clothes and shorts. For visibility reasons, I hang as many garments as possible, because it's easier to see everything and it keeps things from wrinkling. Swimwear I keep in a drawer along with cover-ups for going to the beach, pashminas and shawls, as well as small accessory items.

EBay has a lot of different wardrobe organisation options, just like Howards Storage World, Spotlight, Kmart, Target and Ikea. There are just so many different ideas available if you want to source any wardrobe organising accessories.

During this process, you may discover accessories and garments that you'd forgotten about. You can be inspired and find items that would look terrific together, so lay them out on your bed and take a photo for future reference. If you really want to streamline your time, a 'Look Book' can be created. You could save this on your phone. While this may all seem time-consuming, it will save you a lot of precious time later when you're wanting ideas. How about making it easy to recreate that complete outfit at a later date? You can divide that look book into different sections, such as casual weekend, social occasions, anything you like. There are also apps you can get on your phone to help with this, such as Stylebook and Closet.

You can create a look book with albums in your phone, labelled with the activities you usually do within your personal lifestyle. You can even print off a page of outfits for each occasion and put them into your look book. Think about your personal wardrobe goals. Visualise what's going to make you feel great about your wardrobe.

Chapter 10 - Benefits Of Choice

Walk into your wardrobe and feel good about it, so you enjoy getting dressed and putting those outfits together. There is a great benefit in having choice without the clutter – as long as it's the right amount of choice.

Action Steps

Have a look at your lifestyle now and how it relates to the clothes you have in your wardrobe. Does it all match up? For example, if you are walking every day and then meeting friends for lunch or have more casual social occasions, do you still need all those corporate-type outfits? If you are travelling a lot, do you have enough lightweight layers and garments that don't need ironing and are easy to pack?

A complete overhaul of your wardrobe does wonders for your life and style, because you will feel more organised and it will free up your time and energy for other activities you enjoy, rather than rifling through your wardrobe wondering what to wear.

Resources

Further Information:
If you would like to make your wardrobe audit easier download the step-by-step 'Wardrobe Organising Workbook' (W.O.W.) here:
www.bstyledforlife.com.au/resources
Password is Style50

11.
Be a Smart and Sassy Shopper

As we get older, we realise the benefits of shopping with a purpose, rather than impulse shopping. Unnecessary shopping will only have a detrimental effect on your style and your ability to maintain it consistently.

The Wow Factor

> *"There are three responses to a piece of design, yes, no and wow. Wow is the one to go for."*
>
> – **Milton Glaser**

If you do tend to impulse buy, remember this quote. It could be "wow" this is just what I need in my wardrobe. It could be "wow" this looks amazing on me. It could be "wow" this feels so comfortable and is really going to serve the purpose. My advice is to avoid the "Wow, look at this great price – I'm going to get it!" If you happen to be an emotional shopper, or an impulse buyer, it's always good to have a list for the gaps in your wardrobe. The last thing you need is shopper's remorse. It's important to ensure all the wow factors are there. If they are and what you have bought meets your "wow" criteria, then it can give you a sense of accomplishment.

The Difference Between Shopping And Buying

There is actually a difference between shopping and buying. Shopping is when you go to visit a shop, in person or online, to get more information. I actually do believe in shopping and doing some market research. The more you shop and see what's available out there, the more aware you will be. This will make you a smart and sassy shopper. If you're buying, you're actually handing over your money or credit card and coming away with some goods. It makes sense to do more shopping than you do buying. Doing your market research can save you time and help you know exactly where to shop.

There are shops that carry certain types of clothing and accessories that will suit you personally. I wouldn't always aim for shops that are targeted towards a certain age group. I would find shops that suit your style personality. Think of the words that define your unique personality, for example, if you're a dramatic style personality, think 'edgy', 'modern', 'minimalistic', 'bling' and 'leather'. It's all about you when you're shopping for you. There's so much to choose from, and this will stop you from feeling as though you need to look at everything in all the stores. There are certain shops that cater to different types of personalities. Shops like Forever New and Review cater for feminine romantic styles. Cue and Events cater towards the more classic personality styles. Stores such as Country Road cater for more the relaxed and natural style personalities. This will ensure your purchases will be in line with who you are. It keeps your clothing choices to a minimum, instead of buying everything that's on sale.

Chapter 11 - Be A Smart And Sassy Shopper

Online Shopping

If you don't love the experience of actually physically shopping, or have time restrictions, online shopping is a great alternative. The main three points to remember with online shopping are:

- ✓ Check out the reviews if they have any.
- ✓ Look at the returns policy.
- ✓ See if there is a size guide on their website.

Shopping Dos and Don'ts

- **Do** wear comfortable shoes and easy clothing to get in and out of.
- **Don't** shop on an empty stomach. You won't think as clearly.
- **Do** take a list and have in mind what you want to buy.
- **Don't** buy orphan garments that may be difficult to colour match.
- **Do** take a skirt or pair of trousers with you if looking for a jacket or top to go with that garment.
- **Do** take your colour swatch with you if you have had a colour consultation.
- **Do** check your awards points on your credit card. You may get a nice surprise when you go up to the checkout counter in a department store that accepts awards points.
- **Don't** take a friend with you who's going to distract you if you're shopping for a special event and on a tight time frame.
- **Do** take a friend who can give you unbiased advice, and who you know is going to be helpful and whose opinion you trust.
- **Don't** buy makeup in a department store that is chosen under harsh, artificial light unless you are sure. Makeup is usually unable to be returned once opened if it's the wrong colour.
- **Don't** always trust the shop assistant's advice, because sometimes they may just be wanting to sell what is in and move their stock. A second opinion is great. Your opinion is the absolute best.

- **Don't** purchase anything that's too tight or uncomfortable, hoping you'll fit into it better one day soon.
- **Do** purchase a garment on sale if it's the right colour, the right style, the right shape and great quality, even if it's just a little big. The alteration charge could be worthwhile if it's something simple. Then you've got a great priced garment that's absolutely perfect. I once bought a muslin kaftan, because I loved the trim around the sleeves and hem. I knew I would be able to run it in down the sides, and I changed it into an amazing top. I love to wear it with a belt or just scrunched up at the sides. I took it in about three or four sizes.
- **Do** always try clothes on, unless you're familiar with the brand and the sizing, because sizes do vary from shop to shop, or brand to brand.
- **Do** check returns policies and sizing guides on websites if purchasing from online stores.
- **Do** always check labels for care instructions.
- **Don't** buy an expensive dry clean only garment if it's something you're going to want to wear as a practical day-to-day outfit or garment. Something that's on sale may not end up being as inexpensive as you think if you're going to need to dry clean it all the time.
- **Don't** get carried away shopping overseas, especially if it's something you can buy at home and the exchange rate is absolutely crazy.
- **Do** enjoy your shopping and have fun. Shop smartly and wisely.

You can be your own hunter and gatherer. You won't waste your money if you're smart at shopping, and you'll always be pleased with what you bought if you shop wisely. You can be a very smart, self-aware, self-sufficient shopper!

Chapter 11 - Be A Smart And Sassy Shopper

Action Steps

✓ Take your measurements and know them so you can check website sizing guides if you are purchasing online.

✓ Keep a pen and notepad in your wardrobe so you can jot down any items that you're looking for as you put outfits together.

Resources

Size conversion chart for shopping online or overseas:
https://www.finder.com.au/dress-size-conversion-chart

Link to my personal online shopping channel:
https://shopshare.tv/channel/moana@bstyledforlife

Most of the retail stores in malls have online outlets. Some other ideas for online shopping stores are:
www.asos.com.au
www.aquila.com.au
www.beme.com.au
www.theiconic.com.au

App for creating your own look books:
www.Personallookbook.com
www.stylebookapp.com/
www.personallookbook.com
www.flipsnack.com

Brilliant Life and Style Tips

1. Over 50 benefits – there are many, such as experience, wisdom, discounts…
2. Whatever you start doing, make sure it is sustainable.
3. Appreciate the good people in your life.
4. Stop and think – before you say, eat, agree to, react to, judge.
5. Overwhelmed or stressed – long breaths out and short breaths in
6. Need some balance – breathe deep and slow. Six counts in and six out.
7. Feeling a bit flat – Long breaths in and shorter, Sharper breaths out
8. Keep learning every day. The more you learn, the more fascinating life is.
9. Keep sharing and it comes back to you in return.
10. Find your good people – hairdresser, doctor, dentist, accountant.
11. Girlfriend time is important. Definitely make time for your girlfriends.
12. Laughter and fun times are important – see point 9.
13. Healthy boundaries – 'leaky' boundaries aren't good for anyone.
14. Take a break if you are bored, stressed, overwhelmed, or feel 'yucky'.
15. Everyone is different – appreciate the differences.

16. Self-aware and self-sufficient doesn't mean you can't reach out for help.
17. If you feel like doing something, do it – if you don't, then ask yourself why?
18. If feeling 'yuck', discuss with trusted friend, but don't camp out there.
19. Be honest about your feelings, most of all to yourself.
20. Find a fragrance you love and have a signature scent.
21. Best ever asset, as far as your looks go, is a genuine smile.
22. Notice how you feel in your clothes – this is best indicator of what suits.
23. Once you find a good brand of jeans, stick with these.
24. If bored with your wardrobe, make a few tweaks or join a style challenge.
25. If bored with cooking, learn a new recipe or get Hello Fresh.
26. Find out what works for you and use that – this applies to everything.
27. Be your own best health advocate. It's your body and your life.
28. You can't change what has happened, no matter how bad it was.
29. This is the time of life when you get to choose what is best for you.
30. You can have your own unique style and your own special kind of sass.
31. Fill your cup first. You aren't being selfish, you will have more to share.
32. If everyone is true and kind the world will be a better place. Start with you.
33. Quality communication and connection with self and others is great.
34. What goes around comes around.
35. Trust is not always easy – discernment is about making choices.
36. Great luxury gift for yourself and your friends – a silk pillowcase.
37. Explore your own wardrobe before you go out shopping.
38. Keep in touch with loved ones and friends – time passes by quickly.
39. Think of your best time for exercise and use this. Everyone is different.
40. Incidental activity is good too – take stairs instead of lifts if you can.

41. Pick a day of the week for personal maintenance – a 'me' day.
42. Don't wait for someone else to organise something. Do it yourself.
43. Create special moments in your day that you will remember.
44. Appreciate the beauty of sunrises and sunsets.
45. Read good books for learning, escape, stimulation and conversation.
46. Travel as much as you can. It's a great way to learn about a country.
47. Always take spare clothes and essentials in cabin bag in case your luggage is lost.
48. Moisturising masks on long-haul flights keep skin hydrated.
49. When packing, keep to a similar colour scheme in your travel outfits.
50. Scarves and other accessories can change the look of a whole outfit.
51. Pashminas and scarves are versatile and keep you warm when travelling.
52. Take immunity Ki or ArmaForce Tablets about a week prior to travelling.
53. When packing for travels, the best tip is layers, layers, layers.
54. Take a power board when travelling to plug in phone, laptop, etc.
55. A scarcity mindset will bring you more scarcity.
56. An abundance mindset will bring more abundance.
57. Acknowledge your emotions.
58. Treat yourself the way you would treat your best friend or daughter.
59. If you can stand it, a boost of cold water after your shower is refreshing.
60. Alkanise the body with lemon in a glass of tepid water at the start of the day.
61. Give a stranger a compliment – it could make their day.
62. If you have a good idea – do it…or write it down.
63. If you are looking for inspiration, write, write and write…it will come.
64. Want to take up a hobby? Think of what you loved when young.
65. Perfection does not exist. Getting better and excellence does.
66. Whatever you are doing right now, enjoy it. Give it your full attention.
67. Words are powerful. Taste them before they leave your mouth.
68. There is always a choice – every moment, day, week, month and year.

69. Do it now. There will never be the perfect time.
70. Learn from little children. They don't hold grudges and don't overthink.
71. Have gratitude every day. Everyone says this because it works.
72. You can't be grateful and unhappy at the same time – get grateful.
73. You can't be excited and depressed at the same time – get excited.
74. Have something meaningful to do, something to look forward to, someone to love.

B yourself, let yourself glow
There is more to life than we see and know
Keep learning, keep curious
Stay aware and true
Be thoughtful and kind
And most important of all
Be YOU

Moana Robinson, "B Styled for Life"

"It's truer than true there is no-one alive who is you-er than you."
– Dr Seuss

ABOUT THE AUTHOR

In the Polynesian language 'moana' means ocean. Just as the Earth's ocean is integral to life, Moana believes personal care and development in mind, body and spirit is integral to us as individuals. Moana's goal as a Life Coach and Personal Stylist: "To give each client the tools to have an awareness of the possibilities for their own unlimited potential in life and style".

Moana Robinson is on a mission to empower others to glow from the inside out. As a coach for life and style, she uses her skills to take others on a journey to discover their perfect colour palette, style, wardrobe and more. Being the best you includes what goes on inside the mind and heart, as well as outside.

Combining her experience as a beauty therapist, image consultant and life coach, Moana Robinson has the ability to help people shine by finding that magic combination of colour, body shape, lifestyle and personality. The magic is in unleashing the untapped confidence we keep hidden for fear of standing out.

With a huge amount of life experience, Moana has a passion for helping others using many skills and modalities – each person is an individual and Moana believes in each person being the best they can be.

Moana understands the obstacles that get in the way of living to your full potential, and brings an empathy and kindness to her consultations that envelopes her clients. They know they are in safe hands.

As a mother of two daughters and six grandchildren, Moana feels blessed to have such a wonderful family. She enjoys life on the Gold Coast with her husband Peter, after spending many years in Brisbane. Moana and Peter moved from New Zealand in 1986 just before the birth of their second daughter.

True success comes from following your own path, connecting with people and discovering and using tools that empower you to think, feel and be all you can be.

'B Styled for Life' is about creating the best life and style for the real, authentic you.

ACKNOWLEDGEMENTS

Writing this book came about very quickly after a culmination of many years of wanting to write something I could leave as a legacy. There are so many people I want to acknowledge who played a part in helping me take this step and who have been a huge part of my over 50 growth.

My lovely client Toni Lontis wrote her inspirational story 'Resilience'. I met Toni at a public speaking and presentation workshop I was holding with my friend and business colleague Janeen Vosper. Toni came to me as a client, and then later invited me to Natasa Denman's June 2019 half-day event.

I decided right then and there to take this on. I knew it would be a push, as I had so much going on. It was a whirlwind afterwards, with lots of travelling and working on the go. We had a big overseas trip planned already and an unexpected trip to New Zealand before that to say goodbye to a loved family member. Seventeen plane flights later, and at the retreat in Melbourne I finally started downloading this book. I can't speak highly enough of Natasa and Stu Denman, Viv, Nikola and the team, for all their encouragement and support. They have a system, and it felt so good having this to follow to get everything out of my head and onto paper. Thankyou Toni for inviting me to that event, which was the catalyst for me.

I have so many wonderful friends to thank and wish I could list them all. Each one is very much appreciated. They have supported me through many highs and lows over the years. True friends are gems in life.

I want to thank Mum for always caring and being there. She is like a best friend and I am so proud of her for taking on technology the way she has, which has enabled us to keep in touch. Mum's talks to me about writing really did inspire me. I'm very proud of her.

Sumiko Taksue Eyears for taking photos, including the book cover, and being such a wonderful friend and supporter of my business. I have always enjoyed our photoshoots.

Josephine Keay for the styling and help on some of those photoshoots. It is nice to be able to relax and have fun on shoots with someone as talented as you.

Jennifer Darr of Jen and Jennifer who illustrated this book. Jen has been a long-time friend of my daughter Molly and a family friend. Her mum, Kathy, and I go way back.

My business mastermind groups and peer coaches. I appreciate these connections during the journeys I have taken on later in life.

Kaylene Gray for developing the exercise plan which is part of my online program and was given as a link in this book. A friend and personal trainer extraordinaire.

My wonderful husband Peter and two beautiful (inside and out) daughters, Dayna and Molly, and their amazing husbands. My six grandchildren for being the best gift ever.

There are many people in my world who I appreciate, and the list could go on. Thank you to my readers and my clients, who continue to inspire me and keep me constantly learning every day.

TESTIMONIALS
continued

This book is aimed at mature-aged women who are looking for inspiration and guidance from a coach and personal stylist. I have been a client of Moana's and she knows what she is talking about. Moana believes in looking after the whole package. Life is more than just looking good. It's also about feeling good and confident.

Angie Slater, Life Coach

Moana Robinson is one of those rare people who can ignite the light in people. She helps them feel and look beautiful, whether it is through styling their wardrobe or helping them see the beauty in their lives through her coaching. Moana is a master at bringing out the best in everyone she touches.

Janeen Vosper, Business Coach, Keynote Speaker and Author, Owner at Speech Perfect

I'm so pleased Moana is writing this book. I reached out to Moana, a coach and stylist, to help me organise my life and make life-changing decisions. I'm pleased I did, as I now have more confidence and direction. My journey continues and I feel grateful to have Moana in my life as a coach and friend. Moana is a genuine person who really wants to help women over 50 be empowered to feel the best they can with their own unique style.

Susan Riccobon, entrepreneur

I was almost 70 when I realised that, no matter what age we are, we want to look our best. I knew I didn't. But what was 'wrong'? Happily, I found Moana Robinson! Moana is up to the minute with colour and style advice, and after a revealing consultation with her, I felt a new vista of colour had opened up for me. Moana is generous with her time and really listens. Her professional manner gently guides her clients along a path to a new, personalised, exciting look to reveal the real you.

Robyn Durrington, retired

Moana has a gift for empowering others to glow, inside and out. She achieves this using her skills as a life coach and style coach. Along the way, you will discover the perfect colour palette for you, your wardrobe and your life, together with wonderful suggestions on style and makeup. Knowing how to dress for your body shape is an important component of the session, and this invaluable knowledge enables you to go through your wardrobe and to see your clothes and how they make you feel in an entirely different way. It's as if she taps into your individual personality to develop your own unique recipe for your style and what suits your lifestyle.

All of this newfound knowledge and understanding gives you the confidence to step out into the world, knowing that not only will

Testimonials continued

you feel good, but also look good. B Styled For Life with Moana is a confidence booster and so much more. Her book will mirror her wonderful tips and knowledge and will become a must-read for those wanting to shine in their 50s.

**Toni Lontis,
Author and Founder of Radio Toni and Toni TV**

I have only known Moana for a little more than a year, but it seems almost like a lifetime, as we have much in common and have shared some deep and meaningful conversations and times together. You know that friend you have known all your life and who you share the same morals and values? That's how I feel with Mo. The more I get to know Mo, the closer I feel to her. She is a lovely, caring woman who is very easy to connect with, and it is very easy to feel her big heart, as she is also very generous. Her style and flair are outstanding and she always looks amazing, and so will you when you take her advice. She has this thing she says, "I help people from the inside out" and this is exactly what she does. I know Mo has been through many ups and downs throughout her life, and her life experience has made her both gentle and strong. It seems that now she is in a good place to write this book, and I am sure it will be a very worthwhile read for anyone. Love you Mo, I am so grateful to have you as a friend.

Karen Clark, Business/Performance Coach at Clarkashians and Co

So glad Moana Robinson has written this book on styling for the over 50s. Moana knows how women over 50 want to be styled, which is different to how a 20-something dresses. She is aware that each lady wants a style that reflects their true character. She has a wealth of knowledge for all the different styles, and tips to help each lady find just the right style for her. Now I know that Elegant is my clothing style, it has made each decision so much easier. I no longer purchase clothes that I like, but just don't sit well with me and therefore remain hanging in my cupboard, unused and a waste of money. Moana's style tips are a good investment in yourself.

Kerri Speyers, Life Choices Coaching

I recommend Moana as an insightful, warm, heart-centred human being. With her personal styling business and life coaching, Moana works with her clients on both or as needed. I have observed Moana attract many people in her business, taking them from not so confident and empowering them on their journey. I am honoured to know her as an inspiring woman from our Inspiring Women Today website and group, where she has shared her own personal story. If you are seeking a personal stylist or life coach, she is amazing!

Nikki Taylor, LME Mentors

Moana came into my life over 10 years ago as a business colleague, however it wasn't long before a strong friendship and lifelong bond was formed. Moana is so warm and genuine and gives 100% to everything she is involved in. She loves to help people be their best and she knows that comes from the inside as well as the outside.

Tina Litte, Personal Assistant

DOWNLOAD YOUR FREE PERSONALISED STYLE GUIDE

Do you have too many clothes, but nothing to wear?

Moana takes you step-by-step through a wardrobe audit – from start to finish!

Including:
- ✓ List of what is needed before you start.
- ✓ Simple, step-by-step method for auditing your own wardrobe.
- ✓ No-fuss approach to sorting your clothing, shoes and accessories.
- ✓ Tips for auditing your own wardrobe and saving $$!
- ✓ Advice on how to do a proper clear-out and easily identify any gaps.
- ✓ Help discovering garments you've forgotten about (and how to wear them!).
- ✓ Ways to streamline your wardrobe so you can collate your outfits quickly.
- ✓ Great ideas with a no-nonsense approach to get it done in your own time – no more procrastinating!

Imagine being able to reach into your wardrobe and choose an outfit within five minutes, knowing it will be the right shape, right colour and right style. Zero stress.

Download the keys to your perfect wardrobe here bstyledforlife.com.au/resources Password Style50

HAVE YOU ALWAYS WANTED ADVICE ON LOOKING YOUR BEST?

Make the most of this special discount code for 60% off a Personal Styling Consultation with Moana.

Do want to know what colours complement your skin tone, hair colour and eye colour (and what colours to completely avoid!)?

You'll receive personal advice on colours and styles with a 30-minute, one-on-one online consultation.

The 'Introduction to Colour and Style' session is usually $125, but as a valued reader of 'B Styled for Life', you'll get the same advice and personalised care for ONLY $49. This incredible value is available for a limited time!

Contact Moana today at www.bstyledforlife.com.au moana@bstyledforlife.com.au (mention SASSY 50 Book Special)

HAVE MOANA SPEAK AT YOUR NEXT EVENT

Moana Robinson believes personal care and development in mind, body, and spirit, is integral to awakening to the possibilities of our own unlimited potential in life and style.

As a Personal Stylist, author of 'B Styled for Life – Living with Sass and Style Over 50' and co-author of 'How Becoming a Life Coach Changed my Life', she has helped hundreds of women develop confidence in their own unique style.

She has also helped women and men identify their brand by understanding their personality, values, and the unique essence they bring to their business.

Moana has extensive experience as a qualified Beauty Therapist, Life Coach, Image Consultant and Speaker. Sharing these gifts to help others is a deep passion. Moana writes articles for national magazines and local bulletins, receives rave reviews for her workshops, and captivates audiences as a guest speaker at events across the country.

These events include presentations, workshops and classes for networking groups, real estate agents, charitable organisations, hair salons and their clients, students and coaching groups. Moana's unique style of presentation ensures her audiences receive valuable information they can take with them to be inspired and equipped to look, feel and be their absolute best.

Topics include:

- ✓ The Seven Most Effective Stress Resilience Strategies
- ✓ The Seven Secrets To Styling Success
- ✓ Show Your True Colours With Confidence
- ✓ Discovering New Passion And Purpose After Changes In Life
- ✓ Uncover Your Style Workshops

Contact Moana at www.bstyledforlife.com.au
moana@bstyledforlife.com.au

www.ingramcontent.com/pod-product-compliance
Lightning Source LLC
Chambersburg PA
CBHW031113080526
44587CB00011B/952